BUILDING ASSETS

The Strategic Use of Closed Catholic Schools

CATHOLIC EDUCATION STUDIES DIVISION

Alliance for Catholic Education Press
at the University of Notre Dame

BUILDING ASSETS

The Strategic Use of Closed Catholic Schools

Ronald J. Nuzzi

James M. Frabutt

Anthony C. Holter

Alliance for Catholic Education Press
at the University of Notre Dame

Notre Dame, Indiana

Alliance for Catholic Education Press
at the University of Notre Dame
107 Carole Sandner Hall
Notre Dame, IN 46556
http://acepress.nd.edu

ISBN: 978-1-935788-09-6

Cover design by Mary Jo Adams Kocovski
Interior layout by Julie Wernick Dallavis

Cover photograph: www.skyviewsurvey.com

Library of Congress Cataloging-in-Publication Data

Nuzzi, Ronald James, 1958- author.
  Building assets : the strategic use of closed Catholic schools / Ronald J. Nuzzi, James M. Frabutt, Anthony C. Holter.
    pages cm
  Includes bibliographical references.
   ISBN 978-1-935788-09-6 (pbk. : alk. paper) 1. School closings--United States. 2. Catholic schools--United States. 3. School buildings--United States. I. Frabutt, James M., 1972- author. II. Holter, Anthony C., 1977- author. III. Title.
  LB2823.2.N89 2012
  371.62--dc23
                        2012037233

This book was printed on acid-free paper.

Printed in the United States of America.

CONTENTS

ACKNOWLEDGEMENTS

We acknowledge with profound gratitude the contributions and collaboration of many colleagues in Catholic education who have made this inquiry both possible and fruitful.

We are deeply grateful for the generosity of spirit shared with us by the Archbishops and Bishops and Catholic educational leaders in each participating (arch)diocese: James J. Bock; Kathleen Cepelka; Thomas Chadzutko; The Most Reverend Charles J. Chaput, O.F.M. Cap.; Sister Andrea Ciszewski, FSSJ; The Most Reverend Nicholas A. DiMarzio; Monsignor Kevin Hanbury; Rosemary Henry; The Most Reverend Edward U. Kmiec; The Most Reverend Joseph E. Kurtz; The Most Reverend Richard G. Lennon; The Most Reverend Jerome E. Listecki; Margaret Lyons; The Most Reverend Timothy A. McDonnell; The Most Reverend John J. Myers; Leisa Schulz; Bernadette Sugrue; and The Most Reverend Allen H. Vigneron.

We are especially appreciative of Samantha Reich, an intern in the Alliance for Catholic Education, and her many contributions to this project.

EXECUTIVE SUMMARY

It is common knowledge and widely reported today that thousands of Catholic schools have closed in the decades since the Second Vatican Council. What is not fully known, understood, or evaluated, however, is the disposition of these facilities that once housed schools. With over 6,000 such facilities in the United States, this is an area in need of research.

This study focused on ten Catholic ecclesiastical and geographical units known as archdioceses and dioceses that had experienced a significant number of Catholic school closures between 1965 and 2010. Two related but distinct concerns motivated this study: 1) the risks and benefits of leasing closed Catholic schools to charter schools; and 2) good stewardship of church assets generally. Primary research questions sought to identify the current use of buildings that no longer function as Catholic schools, the number of such facilities currently being leased to charter school operators, diocesan policies and procedures governing the decision-making process in repurposing a school, and the use of income generated by the lease or sale of a former Catholic school. While the study began with the intention of better understanding the practice of leasing closed Catholic schools to charter school operators, the findings and best practices have broader implications for church management.

Multiple data sources were identified and utilized, including publicly available information from the Official Catholic Directory; (arch)diocesan estimates obtained via a researcher-created Catholic Facility Usage Prospectus, which was completed by representatives from each participating diocese; semi-structured interviews; and site visits.

Overall, 25% of school facilities had been sold. Twenty-four percent of school facilities were designated as "unknown," meaning that diocesan officials could not verify or produce valid information regarding the current status of buildings listed in their specific prospectus. Twenty-two percent of facilities had been leased and 18% had been given over to other use within the

> "The current state of limited diocesan knowledge about closed schools is a missed opportunity."

parish. Seven percent of facilities were vacant and 4% had been razed. Leasing arrangements included leases to charter school operators, child care providers, community agencies, corporations, private schools, public school districts, and religious communities. Some creative repurposings included remodeling into residential housing for the mentally ill, senior housing, and community centers.

Only two dioceses had existing, written policies in place that governed the usage of closed Catholic schools and addressed the question of leasing to charter schools. Both also had procedures in place for levying an assessment on rental income to support the overall educational efforts of the local church. A continuum of diocesan processes for closed Catholic school sales or rentals emerged, revealing that some dioceses require broad interparochial consultations and assess all rental revenue, while others leave the entire decision-making process to the local pastor along with any revenue generated. Deed restrictions, ground leases, and other strategic leasing arrangements were utilized in three dioceses.

The data revealed that most participating dioceses did not have a clear policy or set of procedures in place for tracking closed schools or for repurposing them. Central offices as currently constituted did not have the capacity to collect, organize, and mine such data. Closed schools were, for the most part, "off the radar."

"Caring for closed schools is one way that contemporary church leaders and diocesan officials can help advance the spiritual mission of the church by increased attention to the resource these closed buildings represent."

Best practices directed to the diocesan level of church management include: the development of formal policy statements and diocesan structures regarding the care, maintenance, and disposition of all closed school facilities; and the promulgation of diocesan legislation regarding the short- and long-term use of closed school facilities, including conditions for various types of repurposing such as leasing, selling, modified church or civic use, and the conditions necessitating razing.

The current state of limited diocesan knowledge about closed schools is a missed opportunity. Organizing and publicizing currently available space and facilities proactively can be a new and welcome source of revenue for the church, even for her educational ministries. Blanket refusal of all leasing to charter schools does not serve the overall mission of the church, for it may leave idle precious resources that could be used to support all of the church's ministries, including schools. It is difficult to imagine, however, a scenario where it would be helpful to the church's overall mission for a diocese to lease closed Catholic schools to charter operators when Catholic schools are operating nearby. Broad consultations with various stakeholders and solicitude for the currently existing Catholic schools are needed.

The church's spiritual mission and goals can best be realized when adequately supported by her temporal goods and holdings—resources, including property and buildings, that assist the local Church in fulfilling its mission. Caring for closed schools is one way that contemporary church leaders and diocesan officials can help advance the spiritual mission of the church by increased attention to the resource these closed buildings represent.

STUDY OVERVIEW

For over 200 years Catholic schools have served as the "privileged environment" for the Christian education and formation of youth in the United States (Sacred Congregation for Catholic Education, 1977, para. 16). Built largely by immigrant communities against a cultural backdrop of anti-Catholic prejudice and discrimination, the number of Catholic schools grew exponentially during the 19th and early 20th century and served both an educative and protective function for Catholic children and their families (Walch, 2003). Contemporary Catholic schools continue to serve both sacred and civics ends, and have been heralded as "national treasures" for providing a high quality education to an increasingly diverse student population (Spellings, 2008).

Sadly, today, many of these national treasures have been shuttered. The exponential growth that defined U.S. Catholic schools during the first half of the 20th century was followed by a period of decline that has been as long and aggressive (DeFiore, 2011; McDonald & Schultz, 2012). According to statistics maintained by the National Catholic Educational Association (NCEA), the total number of Catholic schools in the United States peaked at 13,292 during the 1965-1966 academic year (Brigham, 1989). Over the next five decades, the total number of Catholic schools declined by 47% to a total of 7,094 primary and secondary schools in 2010 (McDonald & Schultz, 2012). School closures between 1965 and 2010, therefore, totalled 6,198. And, in the three years that have passed since the launch of this study, an additional 409 Catholic primary and secondary schools have been closed across the United States.

The precipitous decline in the number of Catholic schools in the United States has been the focus of many research briefs and policy reports over the past several decades (DeFiore, 2011; Goldschmidt & Walsh, 2011; Hamilton, 2008; Sarocki & Levenick, 2009; White House Domestic Policy Council, 2008). However, in attempting to diagnose, predict, and prevent Catholic school closures, scholars have largely overlooked individual closed Catholic schools as a unit of analysis or topic of study. As a result, little is known about the current condition or use of former Catholic school buildings. To date, there has been no systematic inquiry into the conditions that precipitated or the procedures that govern the new uses of former Catholic school buildings. Neither has there been a comprehensive assessment of potential revenue generated from the rental, lease, or sale of these parish and (arch)diocesan properties and the resultant revenue-sharing agreements. The current

> "In attempting to diagnose, predict, and prevent Catholic school closures, scholars have largely overlooked individual closed Catholic schools as a unit of analysis or topic of study."

study addresses this lacuna in the research literature on closed Catholic schools in the United States.

Amidst this overall demographic backdrop, several high profile school closures and reorganizations in three archdioceses provide interesting cases to further contextualize the current study. First, in 2007-2008, several inner-city Catholic schools in the Archdiocese of Washington, DC, were closed and quickly leased to public, non-sectarian charter schools, a few of which were geographically proximate to existing Catholic schools. Smarick's (2009) case study outlined the timing and mechanics surrounding the process of closing, then leasing, highlighting issues such as the archdiocesan consultation process, finding a charter operator, negotiating leases, and the new schools' staffing and instructional program. Second, Brinson's (2010) case study described the Archdiocese of Miami's experience in closing seven Catholic schools, leasing or selling the facility, and then supporting the opening of public charter schools in their place. The unfolding processes in Washington, DC, and Miami revealed numerous issues that come to the fore in managing closed Catholic school assets: the importance of parish consultation regarding whether or not to consider charter school rental; processes for vetting charter school operators and proposals; negotiation and development of tailored license agreements for facility use; and the need to assess the long-term impact of the charter schools on other parochial schools. Third, in 2010, the Archdiocese of Indianapolis closed two of its inner-city schools, applied to become a licensed charter school operator in the state, and proceeded to manage two new charter schools in the buildings of the recently closed Catholic schools. These schools were the first in the nation to be chartered by an archdiocese through the establishment of a separate and independent corporation, ADI Charter Schools, Inc. The experience in Indianapolis, much like at the other sites, raised questions about strategic use of school buildings and how best to meet the educational needs of students and families, often in economically challenged areas.

"The current study supports the ongoing efforts of church leaders to exercise proper stewardship in relation to property management."

Beyond these particular geographic cases, the current study also supports the ongoing efforts of church leaders to exercise proper stewardship in relation to property management. The disposition of closed churches, schools, and other land holdings represents significant challenges and opportunities for current diocesan and parochial administrators. Recent publications have chronicled troublesome property management issues and even civil and canonical arbitration regarding the sale of church properties and the ownership of funds generated from such sales (Berry, 2011). Extensive ethnographic studies have been conducted in parishes in the Archdiocese of Boston (Seitz, 2011). Since closing nearly 20% of its parishes in one strategic planning effort in 2004, the archdiocese has become mired in expensive litigation and the thorny pastoral problem of several closed buildings being occupied continuously by parishioners, including children, parents, and senior citizens. At present, the Diocese of Cleveland is preparing to reopen 12 closed parishes following the decree of the Vatican's Congregation for the

Clergy, which has reversed the earlier decision by the Bishop of Cleveland to close the parishes (http://www.stcasimir.com/decree.pdf).

This host of issues demands concerted attention and indeed some groups have attended to these concerns. For example, the Conference for Pastoral Planning and Council Development (http://www.cppcd.org), a group involved with parish configurations and reorganizations, encourages a deliberate, analytical approach in facilities assessment concurrent with any pastoral planning. The Conference for Catholic Facility Management (http://www.ccfm.net), a national group of diocesan-level administrators, is actively engaged in promoting a best practices approach to overall facilities management, from construction and remodeling through closure and sale. In this broader context, the current study can be understood as part of the ongoing and growing challenges facing church leaders in the difficult work of maintaining and possibly repurposing any closed church-owned facility.

Caring for the resources of the Catholic Church is, therefore, a primary concern of this study. However, the resources of the church are always utilized to support its overall spiritual mission, and the manner in which these resources are managed and administered can significantly impact the overall mission. In posing research questions focused on the disposition of closed Catholic schools, concerns about management and resources are clearly manifested, but it is the church's overall spiritual mission that is ultimately at stake.

Purpose

The purpose of the study of closed Catholic schools was to examine the current use of Catholic schools closed between 1965 and 2010 in 10 target (arch)dioceses.

Research Questions

The primary research questions guiding this inquiry were:
1. What is the current use of buildings that no longer function as Catholic schools?
2. How many former Catholic school facilities are currently being leased to charter operators?
3. What policies and procedures govern the repurposing of former Catholic school facilities to charter operation?
4. What income is generated by the rental, lease, or sale of former Catholic school facilities and how are these funds distributed and used?

METHOD

The study of closed Catholic schools employed a mixed method research design to address the primary research questions of interest. An original Catholic Facility Usage Prospectus and semi-structured interview protocol were used in this study.

Sites and Participants

A two-staged sampling technique was implemented to determine the most suitable (arch)diocesan sites for the study. First, the total number and overall percentage of school closures between 1990 and 2010 was calculated for the 25 (arch)dioceses with the largest number of Catholic schools in the 2010 academic year. These (arch)dioceses were listed in rank order of school closures, and additional criteria were considered—including experience leasing school facilities to charter operators, presence of publicly funded scholarship programs, and willingness to participate in and dedicate personnel to this inquiry—to identify a targeted and purposeful sample of (arch)dioceses with a significant number and percentage of school closures. Next, 10 (arch)dioceses from this master list were selected to participate in the study: the Archdioceses of Detroit, Louisville, Milwaukee, Newark, and Philadelphia and the Dioceses of Brooklyn, Buffalo, Cleveland, Paterson, and Springfield, MA. One of the original sites failed to complete the first phase of the inquiry and was therefore excluded.

A subsample of five sites was selected to participate in a face-to-face interview and property visit: Brooklyn, Cleveland, Detroit, Milwaukee, and Philadelphia. Interviews with stakeholders at the remaining (arch)diocesan sites were conducted via telephone.

Across the nine sites, 15 individuals participated in interviews, including superintendents of schools, associate superintendents of schools, vicars for education, property managers, engineering consultants, and representatives from (arch)diocesan development offices.

Timeline and Procedures

Initial contact with potential participating sites was established via letter during Spring 2011 and confirmed through follow-up correspondence. The purpose and parameters of the study were outlined and cooperation was sought for a Fall 2011 site visit. Institutional Review Board approval from the University was obtained during Spring 2011.

Catholic Facility Usage Prospectus. Data from the Official Catholic Directory were analyzed to establish the current status of each school within a target diocese. Datasets of Catholic schools from the years 1965, 1985, and 2010 were examined and categorized by school name and address. After examining the data for all three time points, schools were given one of the following designations: open (currently open as a

Catholic school), closed (no longer open as a Catholic school), or unsure (insufficient data to determine current status). A prospectus was then created for each (arch)diocese to verify the "closed" or "uncertain" status of all schools included in the prospectus, and indicate the current use of those facilities that were "closed" as Catholic schools (see Appendix A). Table 1 provides an overview of the categories and definitions used to code the current use of closed Catholic schools in a given (arch)diocese. Data from Paterson (never responded) and Detroit (insufficiently completed) were excluded from this portion of the analysis.

TABLE 1. Usage Prospectus Codes and Definitions

CODE	DEFINITION
Razed	School building has been demolished, no longer exits
Vacant	School building is still standing, but is not in use by any entity for any purpose
Sold	School building was sold and is no longer under the ownership of the parish or (arch)diocese
Leased	School building is owned by parish or (arch)diocese, but is leased to another entity for their use
Church Use	School building is still owned by parish or (arch)diocese, but is used for other purposes (e.g., parish center)
Other	Please select this category and explain if the current use of the building does not fit any of the above descriptors

Site Visits. Dates were secured with (arch)diocesan personnel for the local site visit. Between October and December 2011, two members of the research team conducted each site visit. Interviews were semi-structured and followed a standard protocol (see Appendix B). Prior to beginning each interview, participants provided informed consent (see Appendix C). Interviews were audio recorded and researchers also took notes during the discussion. Interviews typically lasted approximately 45 minutes, ranging in length from 30 minutes to over an hour. Interviews generally took place at (arch)diocesan offices, either in the participant's office or an adjacent conference room. In each (arch)diocese, immediately after the interview, site visits were conducted to closed Catholic school buildings that had been converted to other uses. In most cases, (arch)diocesan representatives provided a list of sites and addresses that would be instructive to visit. In one site, an archdiocesan consultant provided a tour of four former Catholic school sites. Numerous photographs were taken at each site to serve as a visual record of the multiple current uses of closed Catholic school buildings. Arch(diocesan) representatives also frequently provided supplementary materials to the research team, including spreadsheets of recent school closings, copies of pertinent policies, maps of closed schools, and architectural plans and renderings.

Phone Interviews. Following the site visits, a series of phone interviews was conducted with participants from Buffalo, Louisville, Newark, and Springfield. Conducted during one week in early January 2012, these interviews followed the same interview protocol (Appendix B) as used during the site visits. Consent was obtained to audio record the telephone call and either two or three members of the research team were present for each call. These interviews ranged in length from 30 to 45 minutes.

FINDINGS

Data from multiple sources were triangulated to generate the following findings organized by the primary research questions that propelled this inquiry. Digitized audio files from the interviews were downloaded and transcribed. Photographs from each site visit were likewise downloaded and labeled. Supplementary materials such as "lease lists" or maps of charter operators provided by each (arch)diocese were catalogued and filed. Finally, data from the completed (arch)diocesan prospectus were entered into an Excel spreadsheet and coded for quantitative analysis.

In order to code the interview transcriptions, the interview protocol was divided into several main themes: existing policy governing closed Catholic school usage; procedures for usage; specific uses, programs, or initiatives; charter leasing; use of income generated from lease or sale; upkeep and maintenance. These six major thematic areas created predetermined coding categories, which corresponded to the researcher-initiated questions during the interviews and site visits. As a method to distill the data, a matrix was created that cross-tabbed the major thematic foci with the individual (arch)diocesan sites. This streamlined representation of the data allowed simultaneously for cross-site comparison and within-site analysis. The cross-tabbed matrix served as the evidentiary foundation for the identification of primary findings across each thematic area. The research team used the matrix to reach consensus on emerging data patterns.

Thus, the interviews, photographs, supplementary materials, interviewer notes, and the (arch)diocesan school prospectus formed the data corpus for this project, and support the primary findings presented below. Throughout the following section, direct quotations and interview excerpts are highlighted both as a means to illuminate particular viewpoints or to capture a more broadly representative sentiment, all while remaining true to the voices of the participants.

1. What is the current status and specific use of buildings that no longer function as Catholic schools?

Data from the (arch)diocesan prospectus were used to create an overall and (arch) diocesan specific overview of the current status and specific use of former Catholic school buildings (see Appendix D). The overall data indicate that very few of these buildings—even those that were closed in the 1960s and 1970s—are left vacant (7%) or have been razed (4%). Additionally, nearly equal percentages of the overall usage are designated as leased (22%), sold (25%), or Church use (18%). It should be noted that 24% of the overall sample was designated as "unknown," meaning that the (arch)diocese could not verify or produce information on the current status of the building identified in the prospectus. Finally, of the known alternative uses of former

Catholic school buildings, charter schools comprised only a small percentage of uses, outpaced by local public schools and other private educational operations (see Appendix D for a detailed, site-specific overview of current usage).

Interviews and site visits revealed a wide array of current uses of closed Catholic school buildings. While some have been razed and are no longer in existence, remaining buildings that have been leased or sold are now utilized for purposes ranging from early childhood education to public schooling to senior housing. At a glance, Table 2 depicts the most common uses of converted or leased buildings across the nine sampled (arch)dioceses. Other buildings are sold outright, and as property formally alienated from the (arch)diocese, their current uses are wide-ranging and disparate. In St. Mary, Kentucky, a former school building of the Archdiocese of Louisville is now utilized as a minimum/medium security state correctional facility for males, the Marion Adjustment Center. The former St. Anne School in the Archdiocese of Milwaukee now houses a local butcher shop. Undergraduate students entering the academic administration building at Wisconsin Lutheran College walk near the site of the former House of the Good Shepherd School.

TABLE 2. Uses of Converted or Leased Buildings Across Sampled (Arch)Dioceses

USES	BROOKLYN	BUFFALO	CLEVELAND	DETROIT	LOUISVILLE	MILWAUKEE	NEWARK	PHILADELPHIA	SPRINGFIELD
Conversion to Residential Housing for Mentally Ill								•	
Conversion to Senior Housing					•	•		•	•
Lease to Charter Operators	•		•	•		•	•	•	•
Lease to Child Care Centers (Head Start and private)		•	•		•			•	
Lease to Community Agencies (e.g., social services)		•			•				•
Lease to Corporations				•			•		
Lease to Private School (e.g., special needs)	•					•	•		
Lease to Public School System	•	•		•	•		•		•
Lease to Religious Communities (i.e., convent)							•		
Parish Use (e.g., community center, religious ed)			•	•	•				

FIGURE 1. In raised stone lettering appears the name Holy Angels School, still visible above the new signage and entrance for this urban charter school in Milwaukee.

Photographic Record. The site visits afforded the opportunity to compile a visual log of the current usage and status of closed Catholic school facilities. Appendix E is comprised of 12 captioned photos from locations in Brooklyn, Detroit, Milwaukee, and Philadelphia. Together with the photos on the following pages, these depict the variability in usage but many of them also portray stark juxtapositions. For example, the sacred and secular merge in the same frame when one observes the still-visible stone engraving of "Holy Angels School" that now greets inner-city charter school students (see Figure 1). Similarly, other contrasts include a charter school only feet away from the parish's religious statuary (see Figure 2), a popular downtown casino linked via glass walkway to a former Catholic school (see Appendix E, Figure E5), and a public school with a prominent cross on the top of the building (see Appendix E, Figure E7).

Leasing to Charter Operators. Leasing to charter operators was observed in seven out of the nine sampled (arch)dioceses. The two exceptions were the Archdiocese of Louisville, since Kentucky is one of ten states without a charter law, and the Diocese of Buffalo, where it is the Bishop's policy (unwritten) to prevent leasing to charter operators. The other seven sites rented to charter operators to varying degrees.

While some were open to such rentals as an efficient way to make use of vacant buildings, other interviewed stakeholders expressed reluctance to rent to charter schools. One participant expressed that the diocese—with only a few charter rentals—

FIGURE 2. The statute of St. Rose of Lima stands adjacent to Brooklyn Dreams Charter School, a public charter school managed by National Heritage Academies. The building was formerly St. Rose of Lima Catholic School.

is extremely careful about leasing to charters since they are direct competition. One interviewee clarified that while charter school rentals had certainly occurred in the diocese, the newly appointed Bishop would likely not continue that practice. At another site, one stakeholder indicated that there has been recent debate among pastors about leasing former Catholic schools to charter operators. Pastors of parishes that have Catholic schools proximate to the potential charter school have expressed misgivings and concerns regarding the charter school's impact on Catholic elementary school enrollment. The diocesan representative explained that in cases like these, the issue has required intensive discussion at deanery meetings. One diocese stressed that each potential charter school lease is evaluated on a case-by-case basis, and when the available evidence suggests a deleterious effect on nearby Catholic schools, the rental arrangements have not been approved.

Site interviews in the Archdiocese of Detroit revealed one clear upside to leasing to charter schools: the operators sometimes make extensive capital improvements to the school property, including Americans with Disabilities Act compliance enhancements. Similarly, participants from the Diocese of Brooklyn cited that charter operators there have made significant infrastructure investments, sometimes in the $3-5 million range.

Other Specific Uses. Several alternative uses of former Catholic school buildings were described in the site interviews. First, buildings have been repurposed to serve as schools for children with special needs. In the Archdiocese of Newark, closed Catholic schools have been leased by Catholic Charities, which operates such schools. In a similar vein, Brooklyn stakeholders described rentals to schools serving children with special needs and disabilities. These are private schools ranging from Pre-K to high school that are publically funded and designed to serve children with autism, physical impairments, and other developmental disabilities.

Second, some dioceses have found the public school system to be an eager tenant of closed Catholic school buildings. The Diocese of Brooklyn rents space to the New York City Board of Education (see Appendix E, Figure E7). Likewise, the Archdiocese of Newark leases closed Catholic school buildings to public school districts either for classroom or office space, such as the Newark Public School District, the Garfield School District, and Elizabeth Public Schools. The Archdiocese of Detroit does not currently but has in the past rented school space to Detroit Public Schools. In Buffalo, while the City of Buffalo Public School System was engaged in a $1 billion renovation of school buildings, many former Catholic school sites were rented on a temporary basis. The Diocese of Buffalo also leases some former Catholic schools to the Board of Cooperative Educational Services, a regional public education service organization.

Third, some (arch)dioceses reported that early childhood education centers are operating in former Catholic school buildings. These centers may be operated by private, for-profit child care providers or community-based, non-profit agencies. Other early childhood programs are supported with funding from Head Start or Early Head Start; examples of these are operative in the (arch)dioceses of Louisville and Buffalo.

While Table 2 and some of the uses detailed here represent a solid cross-section of current uses of closed Catholic school buildings, it is important to note that other novel uses may emerge. Many of the participating sites noted that there are several vacant school buildings that are available for lease or sale. For example, the Archdiocese of Detroit has a regularly updated website containing real estate holdings available for lease and properties available for sale. As of this writing, two schools were available for sale in Detroit (i.e., St. Vincent de Paul School and St. Luke School) and 23 others were available for lease.

Innovative Repurposing: Senior Housing. One interesting reuse of closed Catholic school buildings has been the conversion of these properties into housing for senior citizens. The Archdiocese of Philadelphia has completed two such conversions and is in the midst of executing the third. The former site of St. John Neumann High School—now rechristened Neumann Place—is home to nearly 80 senior residents (see Figure 3). From an engineering and architectural perspective, the layouts of many old school structures lend themselves well to such conversions as depicted in the schematics located in Appendix F. In another project in South Philadelphia, the Archdiocese was able to expand an existing senior facility into the site of the former Our Lady of Mount Carmel Catholic School (Myers, 2001). The Archdiocese has partnered with consultants to creatively finance such projects through combinations of tax credits, grants, and federal funding from the U.S. Department of Housing and Urban Development.

FIGURE 3. Formerly St. John Neumann High School in South Philadelphia, Catholic Health Care Services now operates this facility as St. John Neumann Place, offering 75 independent living apartments for senior residents.

In fact, the development project at Neumann Place won a community impact award from the Pennsylvania Housing and Finance Agency. An Archdiocesan official explained why that particular project was so significant:

> If we adapt this and build the 75 units of senior housing, not only will the beneficiaries be the people who will occupy it, but the surrounding neighborhood and community will be impacted long term. And that will guarantee that affordable housing will exist for the next 40 to 50 years.

This official further explained that such mission-driven repurposing of Catholic schools essentially demonstrates good stewardship of the Archdiocese's assets. He noted, "The Church hasn't left, we're just serving you in a different way. The Church has educated children here for 50 years. The building now repurposed will serve the elderly for the next 50 years."

Conversion of closed Catholic schools to senior housing has also occurred in the Archdioceses of Milwaukee and Louisville. For example, a residential housing provider known as Burke Properties now operates the historic Mercy High Apartments in Milwaukee (see Figure 4), offering studio and one bedroom units for seniors. The Archdiocese of Louisville leveraged $3 million in funding from the U.S. Department of Housing and Urban Development's Section 202 Program to convert a closed Catholic school—St. Bartholomew School—into senior housing. An area developer, in partnership with Catholic Charities of Louisville, spearheaded the effort to convert the school structure into 24, low cost living units for the elderly.

2. What policies and procedures govern the new use or transition to charter operation of the former Catholic school facilities?

Only two out of the nine sampled (arch)dioceses have an existing, written policy that provides explicit directives governing the usage of closed Catholic school buildings. In both cases, the Diocese of Brooklyn and the Archdiocese of Detroit, the policy centers on leasing closed Catholic school buildings to charter operators.

Diocese of Brooklyn. The Diocese of Brooklyn, by far, offers the most comprehensive and far-reaching directives via two relevant documents. The first is a canonical decree (see Appendix G) issued by Bishop Nicholas DiMarzio of the Diocese of Brooklyn on November 18, 2011, following the visit of our research team. The decree opens by briefly reviewing elements of the 1983 Code of Canon Law, stating that Catholic schools exist and function in communion with the Diocesan Bishop. Moreover, as a result of this communion the Bishop exerts legitimate authority to "issue precepts pertaining to the general regulation of Catholic schools in his diocese" (Can. 807). The decree then proceeds to its primary purpose: to reaffirm existing diocesan policy regarding the leasing of ecclesiastical property to charter schools (i.e., Charter School Rental Guidelines; see Appendix H). The policy—in place since May 2010 and revised in November 2011—is framed by this preamble:

> While it is advantageous for any Catholic institution to rent its vacant property for the long term pastoral and financial support of its pastoral mission, the partial or complete rental of any Catholic facility to a charter school has serious implications

FIGURE 4. Mercy Apartments is a senior housing development on a quiet side street in Milwaukee, occupying the building that formerly served as Mercy High School for girls.

for the long term health of the parochial schools and academies of the region. For this reason, no Catholic institution may enter into any lease agreement to rent either its complete facility or a portion of its facility to a charter school without engaging in the process outlined below. (Charter School Rental Guidelines, 2011, para. 1)

The document then provides detailed steps and procedures for pursuing a rental to a charter school operator (outlined in the following section). Importantly, both the decree and the charter school rental guidelines mandate a specific revenue sharing process for income derived from a rental agreement with a charter operator. Bishop DiMarzio's decree provides the rationale behind the revenue sharing directive, articulating that the policy's "primary objective [is] the mitigation of any adverse consequences that a potential rental to a Charter School may have on the long term health and viability of its neighboring parochial schools and academies" (DiMarzio, 2011, para. 3). The decree continues,

> A constitutive, and, therefore, nonnegotiable part of the aforementioned policy is the revenue sharing of 40% of the proceeds from the rental to those schools which have been identified by the Diocesan Charter School Committee as having been potentially adversely effected by the lease to the Charter School. (para. 3)

Thus, 40% of a parish's rental income from the charter lease agreement is shared on a per-capita basis with parochial schools/academies of the area. The Diocese of Brooklyn has created a vehicle for consolidating and disbursing the funds generated from charter school rental income, the St. Elizabeth Ann Seton Trust. The Trust collects contributions from parishes renting their facilities to charter schools via four equal installments per year. In turn, the Trust disburses per-capita portions of its income to locally affected parochial schools/academies in two equal payments during the academic year. One caveat to this process, however, is that parishes that rent to charter schools must clear any outstanding debt to the Diocese. In some cases a payment plan is outlined, approved by the Vicar for Financial Administration, to cover past debts.

Archdiocese of Detroit. The Archdiocese of Detroit likewise has a policy governing the rental of closed Catholic school buildings to charter schools. The existing policy, while reportedly under examination at the present time, stipulates that when a parish rents a facility to a charter entity, a percentage of charter rental income, estimated to be 15%, is collected by the Archdiocese. This revenue is distributed for special projects, "schools that are still in existence," "or some vicariates have made other charter arrangements so it stays locally within that vicariate." A copy of the policy was not made available to the research team.

Other Sites. The remaining (arch)dioceses do not have an operative policy document specifically addressing the lease or sale of closed Catholic school buildings. That is not to say, however, that no guidance or precedent exists to inform current practices. In the majority of the sampled sites, an implied process was commonly understood among diocesan stakeholders even in the absence of codified procedures (see following section). Some interviewees described the process as "really informal,"

TABLE 3. Major Steps in Charter School Rental, Diocese of Brooklyn

	MAJOR STEPS	DETAILS
1	Initiate Contact and Coordination with Rocklyn Assets Corporation	• Pastor or Board Chair wishing to enter into a rental agreement with a charter school entity contacts the Executive Director of Rocklyn Assets Corporation, a firm which handles property management for the diocese • Rocklyn Assets Corporation provides assistance in securing possible tenants for the school building
2	Written Request to Diocesan Bishop for Permission to Pursue Rental	• If potential charter school lessee is identified, pastor begins consultation with parish leadership • Parish Trustees, Parish Council, and Finance Council provide input to pastor • Parish stakeholders are to consider issues such as: details of charter school rental (e.g., educational philosophy of school, size, curriculum, etc.); impact on pastoral life of parish; impact on other properties, and; financial implications • At the conclusion of parish consultation, letter seeking permission, along with minutes documenting consultation, is sent to Bishop and the Chair of the Diocesan Charter School Committee
3	Bishop Grants Permission to Pursue Rental, Contingent on Analysis by Office of the Superintendent of Schools	• Office of the Superintendent solicits concerns and questions from local parishes, schools, and academies that will be affected by the charter school rental • Office of Superintendent assesses potential district-level impact of charter school rental • Charter school curriculum is reviewed to ensure the educational program is not in violation of the doctrinal and moral teachings of the Catholic Church • List of affected local Catholic schools is compiled and provided to the Bishop for approval. Approved, affected schools are eligible to receive direct financial aid (from the St. Elizabeth Ann Seton Trust) to mitigate the effect of the charter school's presence
4	Final Approval of Diocesan Bishop and Completion of Rental Agreement	• Terms of the lease defined by Rocklyn Assets Corporation including rental amount and schedule for payment • Diocesan Charter School Committee makes final recommendation to Bishop • Bishop informs proper authority of final disposition of the proposed rental • If permission is granted, pastor completes rental process under the supervision of Executive Director of Rocklyn Assets Corporation

while others noted that each request for sale or lease is evaluated on a case-by-case basis. Several others noted that there is no (arch)diocesan policy because the sale or lease of parish property remains a local, parochial concern.

Just as sites ranged from a highly specified blanket policy regarding facility usage to a case-by-case evaluation of rental opportunities, there was also great variability in the required procedures and steps in executing such transactions. It is instructive to examine the poles of this continuum and some of the gradations along it.

Detailed Rental Procedures. First, as already noted, the Diocese of Brooklyn's guidelines for charter school rental are highly delineated. In fact, the Diocese has established a Charter School Committee that is charged with providing guidance during the charter school rental process. This guidance entails: (a) strategically assessing the placement of charter school rentals; (b) monitoring enrollment trends in order to gauge the impact of the charter school on the neighboring parochial schools/ academies; and (c) assessing the long-term impact, both educational and financial, of charter rentals on local schools/academies (Charter School Rental Guidelines, 2011). The committee is comprised of the Vicar General, the Secretary for Education and Formation, the Vicar for Financial Administration, the Superintendent of Schools, the Executive Director of Rocklyn Assets Corporation, and a representative from the Office of Fiscal Management. This committee's oversight is the backdrop against which the four-step process for charter school rental unfolds. Table 3 depicts major components of the process and the key stakeholders involved.

Each charter school is chartered for 5 years. Although the diocese will lease to a charter operator for a longer time period, the charter might not be renewed. In the case of a non-renewed charter, the school property reverts to the diocese retaining all of its capital improvements. A coda to the charter rental process in the Diocese of Brooklyn is a concerted effort to assess the impact of the charter rental. To do so, several data points are monitored by the Office of the Superintendent. One is to chart student transfers out of other parish elementary schools as a result of the opening of the charter school. Second, locally affected elementary schools will conduct exit interviews with departing families. Third, the Office gathers data from pastors via the annual census, capturing the number of students that attend religious education who also attend the charter school. The Office of Catholic Education intends to do an impact study of charter leasing over the next 3 to 5 years in order to better inform its diocesan policies and procedures.

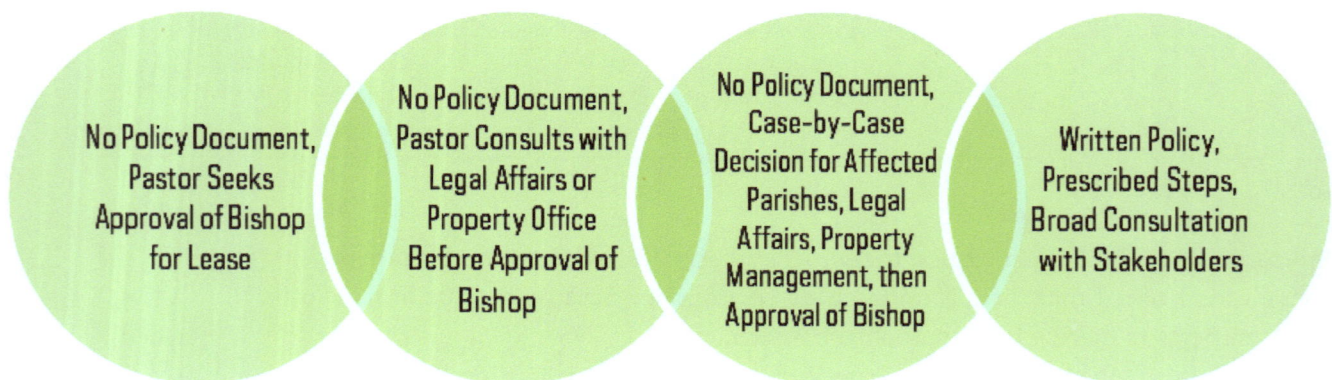

FIGURE 5. A Continuum of (Arch)diocesan Processes for Closed Catholic School Sale or Rental

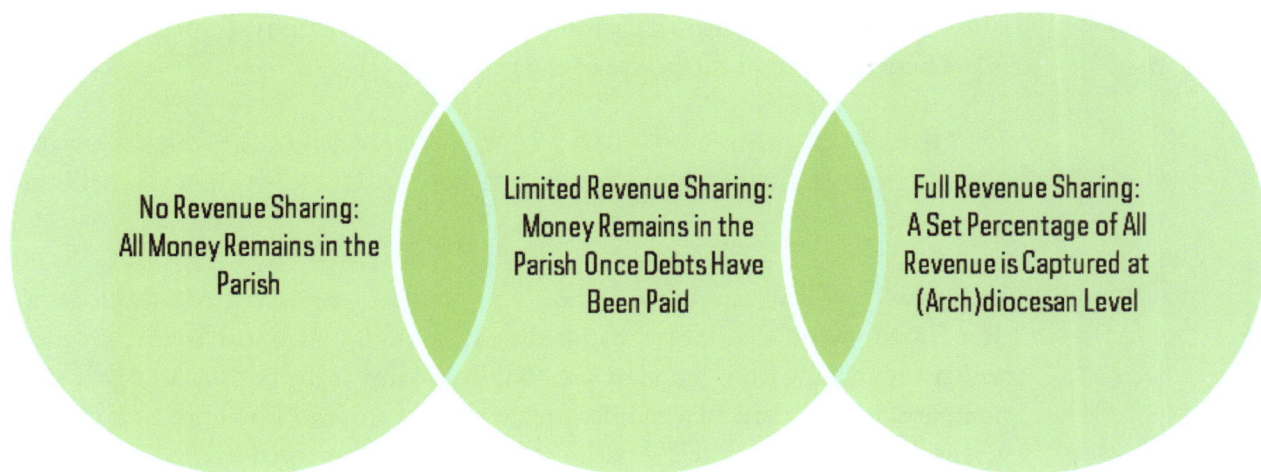

FIGURE 6. A Continuum of (Arch)diocesan Revenue Sharing Procedures

No Revenue Sharing: All Money Remains in the Parish

Limited Revenue Sharing: Money Remains in the Parish Once Debts Have Been Paid

Full Revenue Sharing: A Set Percentage of All Revenue is Captured at (Arch)diocesan Level

A Decision-Making Continuum. In contrast to the highly prescriptive process outlined previously, other (arch)dioceses have a simple procedure wherein the parish may pursue the rental or sale of a closed Catholic school after consultation with the appropriate (arch)diocesan authorities. The particular office or set of stakeholders that must be consulted varied across sites. Gradations along the continuum could be described by the extent and depth of involvement/consultation with diocesan legal offices, property managers, school leaders, and financial officers. Anchoring the opposite end of the continuum from the Brooklyn case, for example, would be direct pastor/parish consultation with the Bishop before renting a school building (see Figure 5). Not represented on the figure is one anomalous circumstance—cited by a single diocese—wherein the pastor enters into a lease agreement without any diocesan consultation whatsoever.

There is a middle ground as well. In the Diocese of Cleveland, for example, a pastor should consult with the diocesan legal office before pursuing a rental agreement. Once at the diocesan level, the legal office confers with both the Bishop and the Catholic Schools Office then renders a decision to the pastor. The individual lease agreement is subsequently executed at the parish level. In the Diocese of Springfield, when a parish wants to lease a closed Catholic school, the pastor and pastoral council consult with the Bishop and the Property Office. In the Archdiocese of Philadelphia, a pastor who wants to lease the former parish school would contact the Vicar for Administration. If it appears that rental to a charter school operator would directly impact nearby Catholic schools, a deanery meeting would be convened to assess the proposed lease. If and when the Archdiocese approves moving forward on a lease agreement, the rental becomes a parish concern and any revenue generated remains in the parish.

Deed Restrictions. Interviews with (arch)diocesan partners revealed an additional consideration outside the discussion of policies and procedures related to the lease or rental of former Catholic school buildings. When a school building is sold outright, three (arch)dioceses indicated that they enact deed restrictions—especially if the parish is still active—to limit future use of the property.

3. What income is generated by the rental, lease, or sale of former Catholic school facilities and how are these funds distributed or used?

Interviews revealed variability in how the income generated from the lease or sale of a closed Catholic school is handled (see Figure 6). At one extreme is a model in which any income from rental or sale simply remains at the parish. As clearly stated by one participant, "parochial monies are parochial monies." The only exception to this arrangement would occur if a parish is behind on debts owed to the (arch)diocese. In that case, debts must be resolved before income is retained at the parish level. According to the interviews, funds from lease or sale remain wholly in the parish in Cleveland, Buffalo, Milwaukee, Philadelphia, and Springfield. In Cleveland, the notion that a portion of the rental income generated from a lease should flow to a common Catholic schools fund has arisen at the level of Priests' Advisory Council, but has not progressed further as of this time.

The other end of the continuum is exemplified by (arch)dioceses in which an assessment is placed on a parish's lease or sale of a closed Catholic school. As mentioned earlier in this report, in the Diocese of Brooklyn, 40% of income generated from lease to a charter school is contributed to a common trust for the support of Catholic schools. If a parish in the Diocese of Brooklyn leases to a public school, the income is assessed at 16%, again directed into the Seton Trust. The Archdiocese of Newark has a similar approach wherein 75% of the income generated from the lease or sale of a Catholic school remains in the parish. The remaining 25% is deposited into a centralized operational fund for diocesan schools. There is movement in the Archdiocese of Newark to alter the ratio to 60% for the parish and 40% for the general school fund. In the Archdiocese of Detroit, a percentage of charter rental income, approximately 15%, is contributed to the Archdiocese, and is redistributed for special projects and to support other Catholic schools.

SYNTHESIS OF RESEARCH FINDINGS

Examination of data across the four primary research questions revealed broader, thematic findings that illustrate the current reality and growing challenges many (arch)dioceses face relative to the repurposing of former Catholic school buildings. These broader findings also inform the best practices that follow.

No Policy, No Matter the Use

The data revealed that most (arch)dioceses lack a clear policy and set of procedures for the transition or repurposing of former Catholic school buildings no matter the intended use. Charter schools received special attention in many locations due to their perceived threat to other Catholic schools, yet few offices had specific, written policies for determining the potential impact of charter schools on the local Catholic school landscape, nor did they have a clear set of conditions under which the sale or lease to a charter school could be authorized. In fact, some participants contradicted themselves by stating that the unofficial policy is "no lease to charters" but the review of the diocesan facility prospectus indicated that, indeed, there were several charter schools operating in former Catholic school buildings. In the absence of a definitive, written policy, many (arch)diocesan offices initiated parish-specific consulting and strategic planning processes on an as-needed basis when schools were to be closed or when the parish sought alternative uses for their former school facilities.

Off the Radar

The lack of policies and procedures that govern the rental, lease, or sale of former Catholic school buildings is symptomatic of a larger organizational and capacity issue relative to the management of school property. Nearly all partner (arch)dioceses stated that the data we requested on the confirmed status and current use of former school facilities did not exist in any systematized form. In fact, this project, and our request for the information, sometimes spurred the (arch)dioceses to organize this information for the first time, and required personnel from several offices within the (arch)diocese to share and compare multiple files and databases. One participant stated, "It was fun; it was a stroll down memory lane." Another superintendent commented on how useful it was to compile the prospectus, noting "It's information that we didn't have before, so I'm grateful to be able to share this with some of our stakeholders, too, who may find it useful." In other cases it became clear that property information existed in unconnected silos; while one department or division maintained a map of charter schools, for example, the office of Catholic schools was unaware of it.

Missed Opportunities

The pervading sentiment was that once Catholic schools closed, diocesan schools officials considered them "off their books" and the facility reverted to a diocesan property manager or to the upkeep of the parish. The lack of a system for maintaining current and accurate information on the condition and status of these buildings results in missed revenue opportunities. Rather than developing a proactive marketing strategy, most dioceses were passive about the sale or lease of facilities and waited to be approached by interested buyers.

BEST PRACTICES

According to canon law and established church practices, dioceses are relatively free within certain parameters to organize themselves for operation in a manner that best suits their particular circumstances. While such practices celebrate the Catholic principle of subsidiarity and honor the wisdom found at the local level as being the best situated to address local concerns, it can often lead to isolation in decision making, with one diocese remaining fairly uninformed about developments in another nearby diocese, even when the sharing of pertinent issues, practices, and concerns could be mutually beneficial. We have seen such isolation in practice: in the current study, not a single (arch)diocese had consulted with another diocese regarding the various property questions that were posed. If any diocese had accumulated experiences, insights, mistakes, failures, successes, and wisdom, these lessons remained unshared. This is regrettable.

While the church has a clearly stated spiritual mission that has endured for centuries, that mission is supported by its resources and can be advanced or inhibited by the thoughtful and strategic deployment of those goods. The land, buildings, and their contents constitute real property that can support the overall mission of the church and help provide the resources necessary to sponsor and direct the myriad ministries now common in contemporary Catholicism. Closed Catholic school buildings currently constitute a significant part of the church's patrimony in this regard.

We recommend that diocesan central office staff exercise an expanded leadership role in responding to this national need for better management of closed Catholic school facilities. Specifically, diocesan central office staff exercise leadership by:

- caring for the resources of the church by managing and closely monitoring the disposition of parish assets such as closed schools, convents, and other buildings;
- actively marketing idle properties, seeking out partners for sales or rental agreements that are mutually beneficial;
- evincing a primary and overriding concern for the mission of the Catholic Church;
- giving priority to Catholic education and by implementing policies that advance the overall educational mission of the church.

Two immediate steps are most pressing if this expanded leadership function of the central office is to materialize. First, dioceses need to develop and establish formal policy statements and diocesan structures regarding the care, maintenance, and disposition of all closed school facilities. Because of the way (arch)dioceses organize themselves with structures similar to departments and department heads, there is usually no clear administrative jurisdiction over a building that once housed a parish school. A parish school naturally falls under the jurisdiction of the parish and its pastor with appropriate connections to the diocesan schools' office and its superintendent, vicar, or secretary, all of whom serve at the discretion of the Ordinary. Once closed, however, such buildings tend to fall into a type of administrative limbo; the schools' office is busy dealing with schools that are operating and the parish may or may not be inclined to investigate potential uses of the facility or even to maintain it or upgrade it in such a way as to make the property appealing.

The central services function of diocesan offices ought to be conceived in such a way as to include this new property cataloging and maintenance responsibility. In larger dioceses and archdioceses, this could expand into a real estate-like office, but in most dioceses it would simply include a database of properties along with a relevant description of the facilities, a plan for its maintenance, contact information for the onsite manager, and some photographic records. In general, diocesan offices could provide better oversight of the church's resources if some centralized record keeping were initiated regarding closed schools. Once collected, such information can be updated annually, and can serve as a critical resource for determining whether or not such properties can or should be remodeled, razed, leased, sold, or repurposed for some other church use. Dioceses should also consider such properties in any diocesan-wide strategic planning processes, examining current physical assets and their status as a prelude to any other planned consolidation, construction, or demolitions.

"Leasing the building which once housed a Catholic school can translate into a regular source of revenue for the parish and diocese, revenue that can be directed to further the church's mission, even its educational goals."

Second, dioceses need to develop and promulgate specific diocesan legislation regarding the short- and long-term use of closed school facilities, including the best conditions for various types of repurposing such as leasing, selling, modified church or civic use, and the conditions necessitating razing. Unused buildings easily and quickly fall into disrepair, often making any repurposing a prohibitively expensive venture. Utility costs alone in some climates make winter maintenance a major expense, whether or not the building is even in use. Over time, unoccupied and unused buildings turn assets into liabilities, requiring a non-trivial outlay of resources for little in return. For these reasons, it would be beneficial for dioceses to delineate the specific conditions for various forms of repurposing.

Leasing the building that once housed a Catholic school can translate into a regular source of revenue for the parish and diocese, revenue that can be directed to further the church's mission, even its educational goals. However, such leasing ought to be done with a view to the church's overall mission and in conversation with other leaders in the local area, particularly neighboring pastors. The church is wise to resist leasing arrangements with those whose work or mission is contrary to church teaching and practice. This practice and policy is already common but is worth stating clearly: no leases, rental agreements, or even *gratis* usage arrangements would be entered into with any organization or person whose public position on matters of faith and/or morals is contrary to the teaching of the Catholic Church. Furthermore, the Code of Canon Law indicates that the final arbiter of official church teaching is the local Ordinary.

Leasing to other educational initiatives such as public schools, charter schools, schools for students with special needs, pre-schools, and day care facilities poses unique challenges. A primary concern of the diocese and parish in this situation should be the anticipated effect, if any, on the currently operating Catholic schools and other educational ministries provided by the Catholic Church. Leasing arrangements of any kind should, at a minimum, not have a deleterious effect on the ministry of Catholic education, Catholic school enrollment, or the potential therein. They should also offer some clear and compelling public good by serving the community and providing welcomed and needed services. Because of the way in which dioceses are organized into parishes, most of which are defined as geographical territories, closing a school building and then leasing it to an external educational provider can impact several parish communities, multiple schools, and several public school jurisdictions. Therefore, such leasing arrangements should be preceded by a diocesan-mandated consultation, including the pastors and parish councils of all involved parishes. Such a consultation should be more than a listening session; it should be informed by demographic and financial data and driven by the overall educational and evangelical mission of the church. While such consultations do not guarantee unanimity on every leasing agreement, they do constitute a vehicle within which concerns and ideas can be expressed, heard, evaluated, and balanced with competing views.

Innovative and strategic leasing opportunities should be fully vetted as a way to protect the church's interest into the future while still creating an attractive leasing situation to potential clients. For example, ground leases, in which tenants sign an extended lease to develop a property during the lease period, are a potential option. Triple net leases are another viable consideration. In these lease agreements, the tenant assumes the costs of the asset, such as building maintenance, taxes, and insurance, during the lease period. These two lease examples demonstrate vehicles for protecting the church's long-term interest while providing a win-win situation in a business context.

> "The policy of levying a diocesan assessment on such rental income to go towards supporting scholarships for students to attend Catholic schools . . . appears to be a new and somewhat felicitous source of revenue for Catholic education."

The policy of requiring rental income received by a parish to be applied first to any outstanding diocesan debt seems reasonable and just. The policy of levying a diocesan assessment on such rental income to go towards supporting scholarships for students to attend Catholic schools or for supporting Catholic schools in general appears to be a new and somewhat felicitous source of revenue for Catholic education. Individual dioceses, in consultation with their respective priests' councils and diocesan finance commissions, should consider a diocesan policy that directs a specified percentage of rental income, after the retiring of any outstanding diocesan debt, to a central scholarship fund for tuition assistance for students with demonstrated need to attend Catholic schools.

Sale of church property, because it is irreversible, ought to be done with great deliberation, respecting the various provisions of local and universal church law regarding its disposition. Dioceses are wise to issue strong and clear directives to pastors and parish councils regarding selling church property, especially in those circumstances where titles and deeds no longer include any diocesan officials. Deed restrictions

TABLE 4. Summary of Key Action Steps

1. Develop and establish diocesan policies and structures for the care, maintenance, and disposition of all closed schools	• Appoint central office staff to be the primary resource for gathering, organizing, and maintaining all building-specific information for closed school buildings • Create a database of property-related information for all closed facilities, including detailed descriptions and architectural plans; a current, professional physical plant assessment detailing strengths and weaknesses; a maintenance plan with estimated costs; onsite manager contact information; and a photographic record • Make database available for decision-making processes and strategic planning when considering selling, leasing, razing, or otherwise repurposing the building
2. Develop and promulgate diocesan legislation regarding the short- and long-term use of closed school facilities, including conditions for various types of repurposing such as leasing, selling, modified church or civic use, and the conditions necessitating razing	Leasing • Assure there is no conflict with church teaching and practice • For a school or other educational enterprise, gauge the likely effects on local Catholic schools via a broad consultation with pastors and parish representatives • Pay any and all outstanding debts to the diocese first with any revenue generated from the lease • Consider levying a special assessment on rental income to support scholarship funds for students in need to attend Catholic schools • Consider ground leases, triple net leases, or other strategic leasing arrangements as a way to protect the church's long-term interests Selling • Assure there is no conflict with church teaching and practice • Abide by the provisions of canon law and local diocesan policy • Consult broadly with stakeholders, including pastors and parish representatives • Consider deed restrictions to protect future interests • Fully disclose terms of the sale Repurposing to an External Agent • Assure there is no conflict with church teaching and practice • If intermittent usage becomes regular, consider leasing Razing • Attend to environmental and safety concerns, especially those related to asbestos abatement • Consult a diocesan-approved list of service providers for expert special services in the areas of structural engineering, risk management, demolition, safety, and insurance

TABLE 5. Summary of (Arch)Diocesan Best Practices for Management of Closed Catholic School Facilities

1. Designate staff with specific responsibilities for the collection and maintenance of building records and relevant, building-specific information for all closed schools.

2. Organize and make accessible a database or website of these data to all decision-makers with responsibility for strategic planning, diocesan planning, and school reorganizations and consolidations.

3. Actively pursue leasing arrangements and rental income through the services of a licensed real estate broker or other qualified agent. Consider ground leases, triple net leases, or other strategic leasing arrangements when feasible.

4. Steadfastly refuse leasing arrangements when they pose a threat to existing Catholic schools or other church sponsored educational programs.

5. Communicate frequently with the office of the bishop or his vicar regarding the suitability of potential renters.

6. Consult broadly with all involved stakeholders, including pastors and parishioners, prior to the execution of any lease or sale of church property. Consider deed restrictions as a part of any sale of church property.

7. Levy an assessment, agreed to by the presbyteral council or similar body, upon rental income from closed Catholic schools, to finance scholarships to Catholic schools for students with manifest financial need.

should also be considered as a way to protect the church's interest in future or repeated sales of the property. Required notifications of various stakeholders, consultations with neighboring pastors and parishes, and full disclosure of terms to the diocese should be standard operating procedures.

Repurposing a closed school building for other use by the parish should normally be a parish decision. Intermittent usage for civic or social purposes, too, remains a parish concern, but sustained usage in such an effort could be a sufficient reason to pursue other leasing arrangements that might prove mutually beneficial for the parish and the civic community.

Razing any building necessitates multiple conversations including real estate specialists, structural engineers, demolition experts, and environmental inspectors, to name but a few. Dioceses can help facilitate needed demolitions by having pre-approved service providers in each area and by defining the steps of a decision-making process that results in specified modifications and upgrades to support further internal usage or leasing, sale, or demolition.

In order to assist parishes and dioceses in their long-range planning and out of respect and solicitude for the important mission of the church and her many valuable ministries, Table 4 provides a summary of the key actions steps to be taken at the diocesan level. Table 5 summarizes the best practices discovered during the course of the study and Appendix I provides a checklist for (arch)diocesan self-assessment in regard to key best practices.

CONCLUSION

This study has adopted a best practices view to the management of church property, investigating the current state of affairs relative to the thousands of closed Catholic school buildings in the United States. In this effort, the study is similar both in focus and purpose to many other initiatives currently underway in American Catholicism. The National Leadership Roundtable on Church Management (www.nlrcm.org) has conducted similar studies for dioceses focused on business operations such as human resource management and financial management, knowing that the quality of the church's temporal and business operations is directly related to her ability to accomplish her spiritual goals. In a similar manner, The Krusinski Organization, an architectural firm in Chicago, has undertaken a comprehensive facility assessment of all school properties in the Archdiocese of Milwaukee. The Mid-Atlantic Consortium, a group of dioceses on the East Coast, is engaged in a series of best practices efforts to enhance business operations. The professional services of such colleagues and others across the United States demonstrate a clear and growing trend that improvement in church management in every area is a broadly shared concern.

> "Organizing and publicizing currently available space and facilities proactively can be a new and welcome source of revenue for the church, even for her educational ministries."

Despite increased focus on professional services to improve management practices in the church broadly, the current state of limited diocesan knowledge about closed schools is a missed opportunity. Organizing and publicizing currently available space and facilities proactively can be a new and welcome source of revenue for the church, even for her educational ministries.

The question of leasing closed Catholic schools to charter operators is a divisive question today, often producing visceral responses. Many veteran Catholic educators and church leaders consider charter schools competition and free competition at that. As tuition-free alternatives to Catholic and other private schools, charter schools have a decided advantage in attracting those who are interested in an education different from what is provided in the local public school.

Blanket refusal of all leasing to charter schools, however, does not serve the overall mission of the church, and may very well leave idle precious resources that could be used to support all of the church's ministries, including schools. Thus, a strategic, thoughtful, and well-executed leasing arrangement could help ameliorate social conditions in a neighborhood, provide a modest source of revenue to a parish, help fund a diocesan tuition assistance scholarship program for students with demonstrated need, retire diocesan debt, and all the while not negatively impact Catholic school enrollment. On the contrary, some such arrangement can actually benefit the church and her educational ministries if done with proper consultation and planning.

On the other hand, as free alternatives to public schools, charter schools can constitute a serious threat to Catholic schools, especially in the urban core. Absent strong, state-wide voucher programs, tuition tax credits, or other legislative vehicles financially supporting parental choice in education, Catholic schools have experienced difficulty competing with charter schools. It is hard to imagine a scenario where it would be helpful to the church's overall mission for a diocese to wholesale or without due process lease closed Catholic schools to charter operators when there were Catholic schools operating nearby. At the same time, it is also hard to imagine a scenario where it would be helpful to wholesale or without due process decide not to lease Catholic schools to charter operators if revenue generated from such a lease could advance the overall educational mission of the Church and help revitalize existing Catholic schools.

The church's spiritual mission and goals can best be realized when adequately supported by her resources. Caring for closed Catholic schools is one way that contemporary church leaders and diocesan officials can help advance the spiritual mission of the church by increased attention to the resource these closed buildings represent.

REFERENCES

Berry, J. (2011). *Render unto Rome: The secret life of money in the Catholic church.* New York: Random House.

Brigham, F. H. (1989). *United States Catholic elementary and secondary schools 1988-1989. A statistical report on school, enrollment, and staffing.* Washington, DC: National Catholic Educational Association.

Brinson, D. (2010). *Turning loss into renewal: Catholic schools, charter schools, and the Miami experience.* Washington, DC: Seton Education Partners.

DeFiore, L. (2011). *Story of the storm: Catholic elementary schools from the 1960s to the present.* Arlington, VA: National Catholic Educational Association.

Goldschmidt, E. P., & Walsh, M. E. (2011). *Sustaining urban Catholic elementary schools: An examination of governance models and funding strategies.* Chestnut Hill, MA: Boston College.

Hamilton, S. W. (Ed.). (2008). *Who will save America's urban Catholic schools?* Washington, DC: Thomas B. Fordham Institute.

McDonald, D., & Schultz, M. M. (2012). *The annual statistical report on schools, enrollment, and staffing: United States Catholic elementary and secondary schools 2011-2012.* Arlington, VA: National Catholic Educational Association.

Myers, J. (2011, March 24). St. Monica Manor undergoes expansion. *The South Philly Review.* Retrieved from http://www.southphillyreview.com

Sacred Congregation for Catholic Education. (1977). *The Catholic school.* Washington, DC: United States Catholic Conference.

Sarocki, S., & Levenick, C. (2009). *Saving America's urban Catholic schools: A guide for donors.* Washington, DC: Philanthropy Roundtable.

Seitz, J. (2011). *No closure: Catholic practice and Boston's parish shutdowns.* Cambridge, MA: Harvard University Press.

Smarick, A. (2009). *Catholic schools become charter schools: Lessons from the Washington experience.* Washington, DC: Seton Education Partners.

Spellings, M. (2008, January 28). Statement from Secretary Spellings on Catholic schools week [Press release]. Retrieved from http://www2.ed.gov/news/pressreleases/2008/01/01282008.html

Walch, T. (2003). *Parish school: American Catholic parochial education from colonial times to the present.* Washington, DC: National Catholic Educational Association.

White House Domestic Policy Council. (2008). *Preserving a critical national asset: America's disadvantaged students and the crisis in faith-based urban schools.* Washington, DC: U.S. Department of Education.

APPENDIX A

Sample of (Arch)diocesan Prospectus

Roman Catholic Diocese of Buffalo
Catholic School Prospectus
Closed Catholic Schools 1965-2010

OVERVIEW

The total number of Catholic schools in the United States peaked at 13,292 during the 1965-1966 academic year. Over the next five decades, the total number of Catholic schools declined by 47% to the current total of 7,094 primary and secondary schools. School closures between 1985 and 2010 (n = 2,246) account for nearly 40% of all school closures. Many of these closed Catholic school buildings are still in use, but little is known about the specific programs or initiatives they house, the conditions and procedures that precipitated and govern these new uses, or the potential revenue generated from the rental, lease, or sale of these parish and (arch)diocesan properties.

The purpose of this study is to use historical data from the Official Catholic Directory to identify the Catholic schools that have closed between 1965 and 2010, and to partner with (arch)diocesan leaders to examine the current use of these former Catholic school buildings.

METHOD

In this study data from the Official Catholic Directory were analyzed to establish the current status of each school within a target diocese. Datasets of Catholic schools from the years 1965, 1985, and 2010 were examined and categorized by school name and address. After examining the data for all three time points, schools were given one of the following designations: open (currently open as a Catholic school), closed (no longer open as a Catholic schools), unsure (insufficient data to determine current status). This study targets schools that fall in the "closed" or "uncertain" categories.

DIOCESAN DEMOGRAPHICS

	1965	1985	2010	Net Change 1965-2010
Number of Schools	236	150	71	-165
Student Enrollment	99,079	37,293	19,082	-79,997
Number of Staff	2,795	2,348	1,950	-845

*Demographic information will be revised based on the information provided by each (arch)diocese.

Questions: Please call or Email Fr. Ron Nuzzi at 574-631-7730 or rnuzzi@nd.edu

INSTRUCTIONS

We are now reaching out to you, our diocesan partners, to verify and confirm the analysis we conducted using the Official Catholic Directory data. Instructions for completing the verification of our analysis are included below.

STEP 1. Verifying Status

The first step of the confirmation process pertains to the current status of the schools listed in the table below. Based on our preliminary analysis, it is our assumption that schools listed here are closed as Catholic schools, and so we have already placed a check mark (✓) in the "closed" column. If the school is indeed closed, no further action is needed for step 1. If the school is NOT CLOSED as a Catholic school, please indicate this by placing a check mark (✓) in the "open" column. See example below.

STEP 2. Identifying Use

The second step of the confirmation process pertains to the current use of closed schools. For each closed school, please select the "Use Code" that best describes the current use of the closed Catholic school. Please write your selection in the space provided. See example below.

Razed: School building has been demolished or no longer exists.
Vacant: School building is still standing, but it is not in use by any entity for any purpose.
Sold: School building was sold and is no longer under the ownership of a parish or diocese.
Leased: School building is owned by parish or diocese, but is leased for their use.
Church Use: School building is still owned by parish or diocese, but is used for other purposes (e.g., parish center).
Other: Please select this category and explain if the current use of the building does not fit any of the above descriptors.

EXAMPLE				STATUS		USE
NAME	MOST RECENT ADDRESS	CITY	ZIP	CLOSED	OPEN	RAZED, VACANT, SOLD, LEASED, CHURCH USE, OTHER
St. Joseph Catholic Grade School	123 Main Street	Anywhere	12345	✓		Leased to community org.
St. Joseph Catholic High School	321 Center Street	Anywhere	12345	✓	✓	

Questions: Please call or Email Fr. Ron Nuzzi at 574-631-7730 or rnuzzi@nd.edu

CLOSED SCHOOL STATUS

According to our analysis, the following schools are no longer open and operating as a Catholic school in the Diocese of Buffalo. Please confirm the STATUS and USE of these facilities per the instructions provided above.

| NAME | MOST RECENT ADDRESS | CITY | ZIP | STATUS | | USE |
				CLOSED	OPEN	RAZED, VACANT, SOLD, LEASED, CHURCH USE, OTHER
All Saints	127 Chadduck Ave.	Buffalo	14207	✓		
Archbishop Carroll High School	1409 E. Delavan Ave.	Buffalo	14215	✓		
Ascension	168 Robinson St.	North Tonawanda	14120	✓		
Assumption	Transit Rd.	Swormville	14146	✓		
Assumption (Polish)	435 Amherst St.	Buffalo	14207	✓		
Assumption (Polish)	Brown St.	Albion	14411	✓		
Assumption of the Blessed Virgin Mary	*No address given	Lancaster	14085	✓		
Basilica of Our Lady of Victory	767 Ridge Rd.	Lackawanna	14218	✓		
Bishop Colton High School	128 Wilson St. (12)	Buffalo	14212	✓		
Bishop Duffy High School	520 66th St.	Niagara Falls	14304	✓		
Bishop Fallon High School	1238 Main St.	Buffalo	14209	✓		
Bishop Gibbons High School	1110 Payne Ave.	North Tonawanda	14120	✓		

Questions: Please call or Email Fr. Ron Nuzzi at 574-631-7730 or rnuzzi@nd.edu

APPENDIX B
Site Visit / Interview Guide

I. EXISTING DATA	Key Informants' Contact Information	Name Title Role/Relevance to Catholic school facilities
	Diocesan-Verified Facility Closures and Current Use	Data on Catholic school closures derived from the Official Catholic Directory (OCD) is compiled, then verified by diocesan partners. Diocesan partners provide information on current usage of closed Catholic school facilities.
	Policies and Procedures	Copies of any existing diocesan policies and/or procedures that govern the usage of closed Catholic school buildings are requested during site visit.

II.
SEMI-
STRUCTURED
INTERVIEWS
	Interview Protocol
	
	Opening
	
	• Thank you for participation and collaboration
	• Outline purpose of larger study and of this visit
	• Address any questions about the Closed Catholic School Prospectus that they have completed
	• Confirm receipt of signed consent, including permission to take notes, record, take photos of buildings
	• Opening grand tour questions: What is the general feeling right now in the central office about Catholic schools? What's the current state of affairs and what are most people spending their time on?
	
	Key Questions
	
	1. What policies and procedures govern the usage of closed Catholic school buildings?
	  a. If written, request a copy.
	  b. If written policy does not exist, ask informant to describe what typically transpires in determining the usage of facilities.
	
	2. What is the primary, current usage of closed Catholic school buildings? Use completed prospectus, if available, to facilitate this discussion.
	  a. Offer options and solicit commentary on each:
	    i. Vacant
	    ii. Razed
	    iii. Sold
	    iv. Leased/Rented
	    v. Other church/Parish use		

II.
SEMI-
STRUCTURED
INTERVIEWS
	3. Are any specific programs or initiatives housed in closed Catholic school buildings? Provide examples.
	
	4. Are any closed Catholic school buildings leased to a charter operator?
	
	   a. What policies and procedures govern the transition to charter operation of the former Catholic school facilities?
	
	5. What income is generated by the rental, lease, or sale of former Catholic school facilities?
	
	   a. How are these funds distributed and used?
	
	6. Who is responsible for the upkeep and maintenance of these facilities?
	
	7. What lays ahead for your Catholic schools in the next year or two? Any new plans on the horizon?
	
	8. Any other comments, questions, or insights?
	
	Closing
	
	- Timeline for study completion and next steps
	- Contact information for follow-up or additional clarification
	- Request verification of any site-specific write-up; member checking
	- Thank you for participation and collaboration

III. ONSITE TOURS OR PROPERTY VISITS	Visits to Individual Closed Catholic School Sites - School Name and Location - History and Dynamics surrounding Closure - General Description and Current Use - Photographs

APPENDIX C
Consent Form for Study Participation

Dear Catholic School Stakeholder,

Thank you for your ongoing interest and partnership in our Catholic School Facilities Study (CSFS). Our research efforts continue as we organize our information regarding the current disposition of buildings that once housed schools.

As you know, we have selected your (arch)diocese as an exemplary case study site for the Catholic School Facilities Study (CSFS). We would like to meet with you to discuss the results of our initial analysis of the school buildings in your (arch)diocese that no longer house Catholic schools. We are primarily interested in understanding the policies and procedures that govern the closure and new uses of these facilities.

Portions of our meeting will be audio-recorded and transcribed for analysis. Excerpts and quotes from our conversation may be used in our final report. As such, you may be identified by name and position title in our report unless you would prefer to remain anonymous. We do not predict that our conversation about these school buildings will precipitate any discomfort or inconvenience.

Your decision to provide or refuse consent for this project will in no way affect your relations with the University of Notre Dame or the Alliance for Catholic Education. If you decide to provide your consent to participate, you are free to withdraw it at any time.

If you have any questions or concerns regarding this research project, your consent, or your participation, please contact me at the information below. A signed copy of this form will be provided to you for future reference.

_____

Your signature indicates that you understand the purposes of the Catholic School Facility Study described above, and are providing your consent to participate.

_____

Name (please print)   Date

_____

Signature   Initial here if you will allow us to use your name in our final report.

_____

Researcher Signature: Rev. Ronald J. Nuzzi, Ph.D.   Date
574-631-7730; rnuzzi@nd.edu

Data on Current Catholic School Facility Usage

SCHOOL FACILITY USAGE STUDY

Total School Closures: 1,047

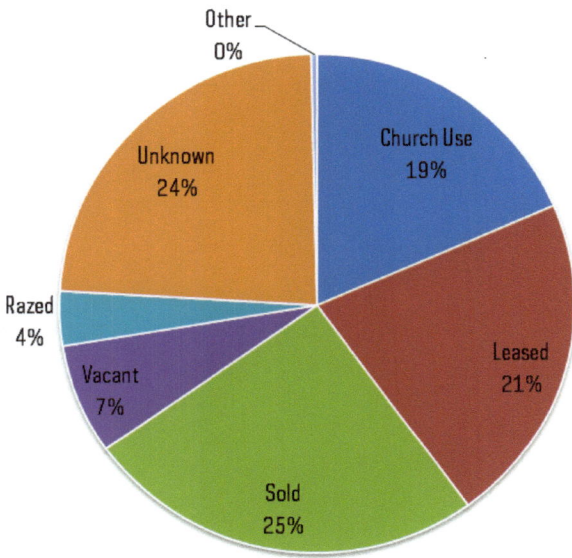

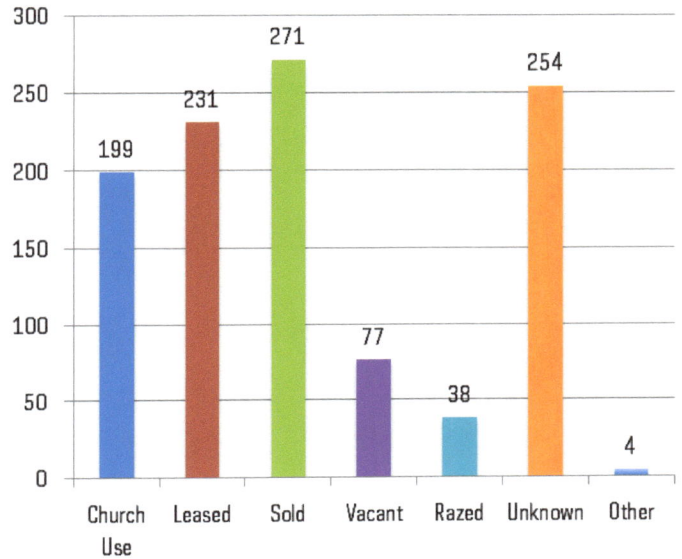

FIGURES D1 and D2. Total Closed Catholic School Facility Use by Percentage and by Frequency Count

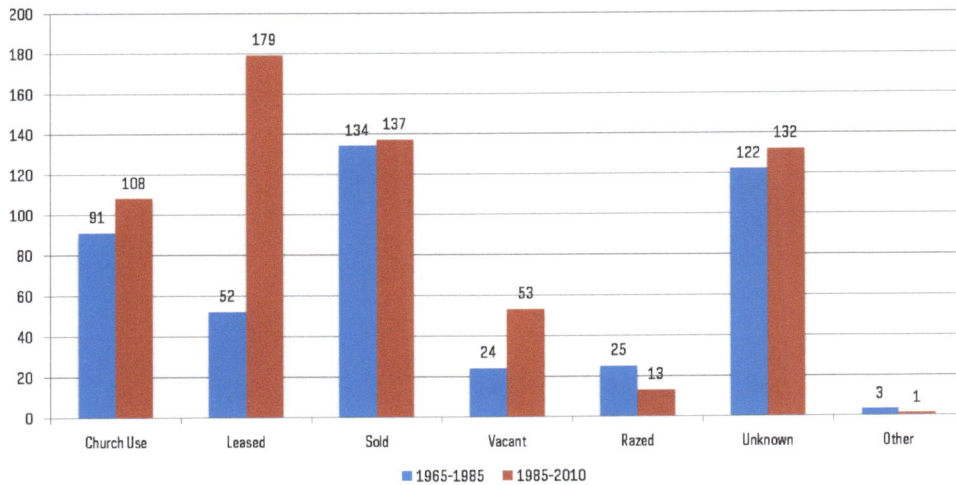

FIGURE D3. Total Catholic School Closures by Decade Window

DIOCESE OF BROOKLYN

Total School Closures: 142

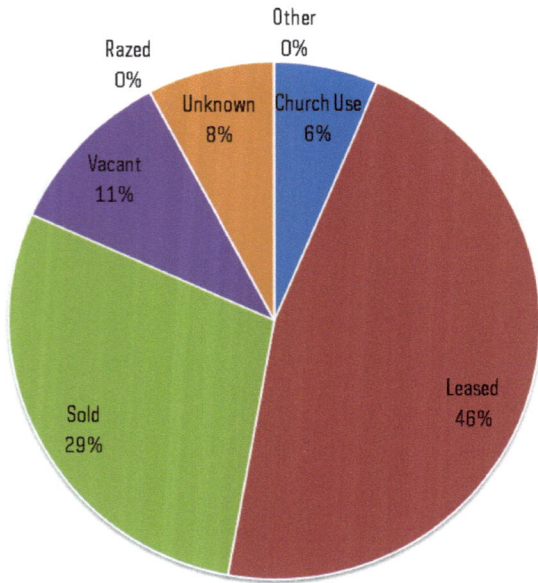

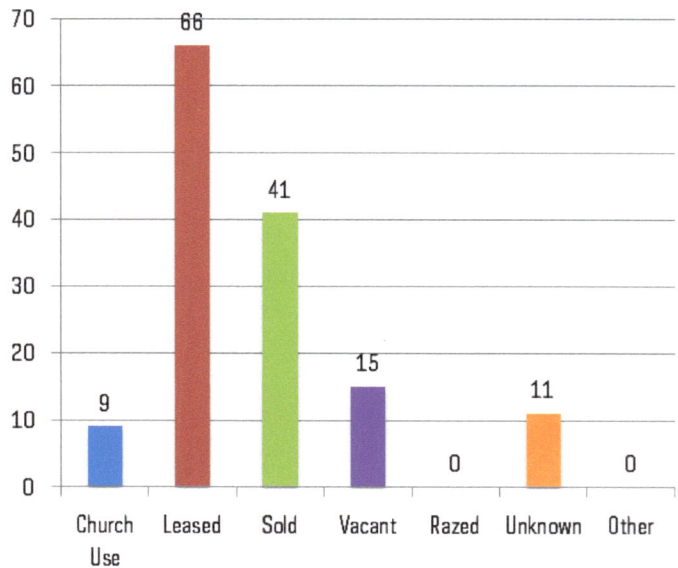

FIGURES D4 and D5. Total Closed Catholic School Facility Use by Percentage and by Frequency Count

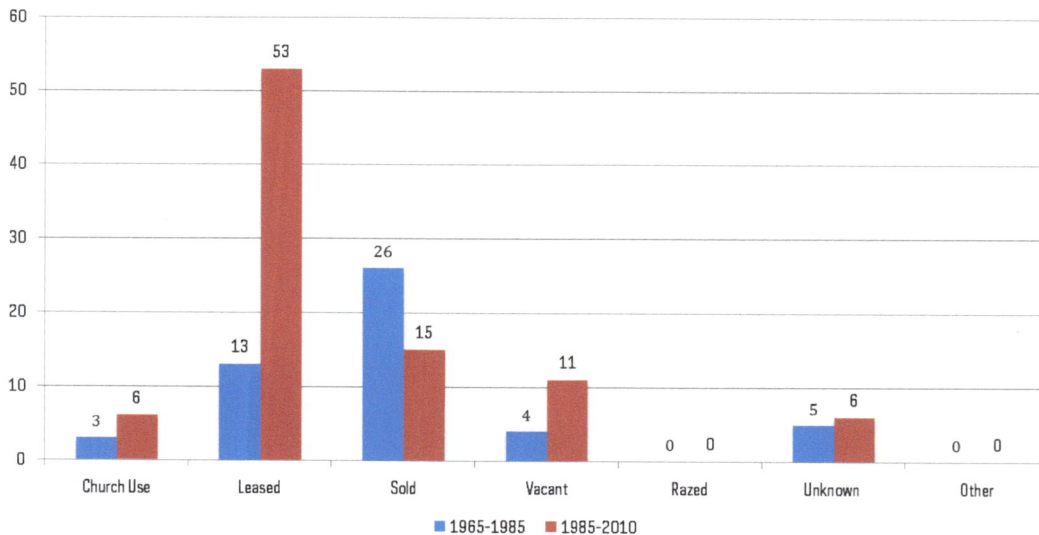

FIGURE D6. Total Catholic School Closures by Decade Window

Notes: Seven (7) former Catholic schools had been leased to charter schools, nineteen (19) had been leased to the New York City Department of Education, and a total of fifty-three (53) facilities had been leased to educational institutions such as day care or special education programs.

DIOCESE OF BUFFALO

Total School Closures: 167

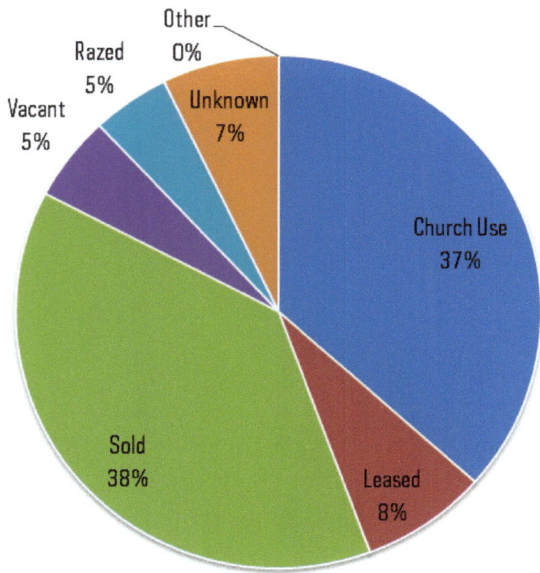

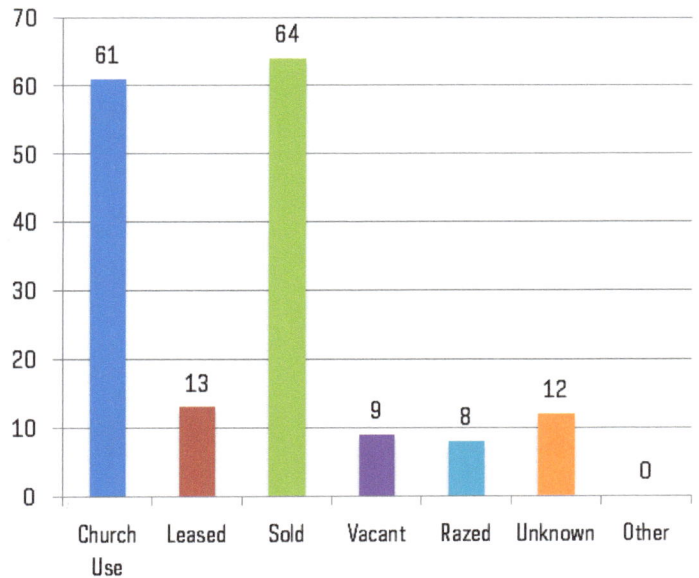

FIGURES D7 and D8. Total Closed Catholic School Facility Use by Percentage and by Frequency Count

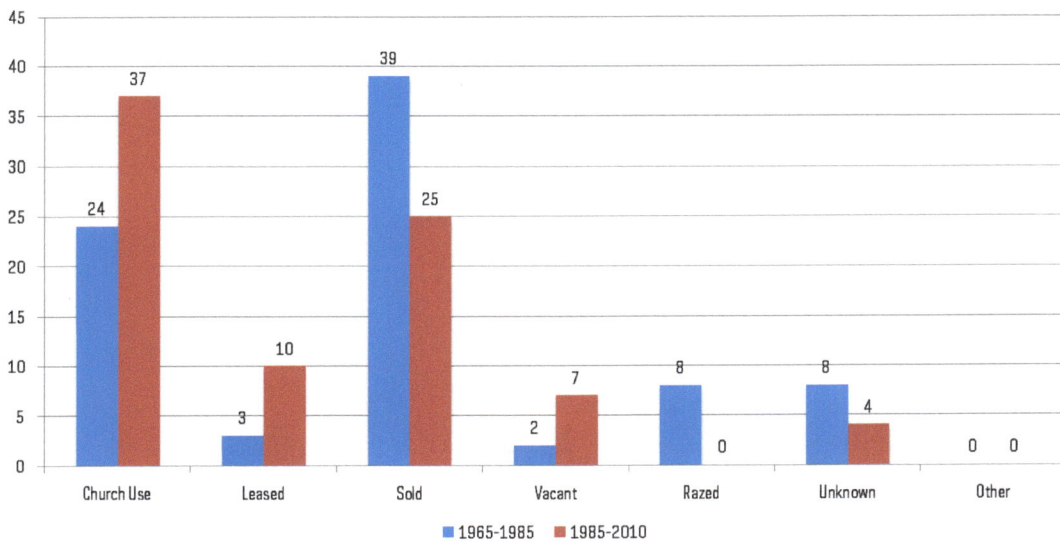

FIGURE D9. Total Catholic School Closures by Decade Window

Notes: Twelve (12) of the thirteen (13) buildings leased to other entities (92%) were leased to educational organizations. None were leased to charter schools.

DIOCESE OF CLEVELAND

Total School Closures: 122

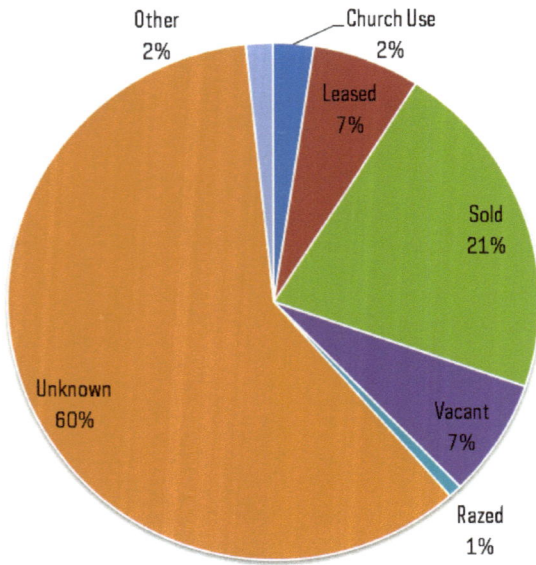

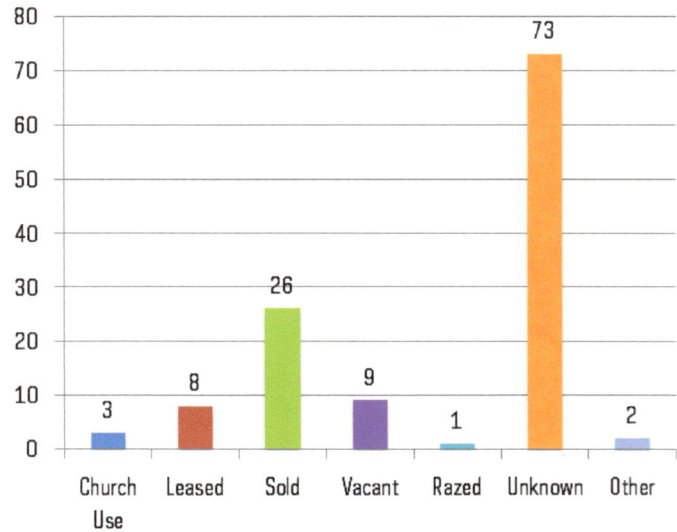

FIGURES D10 and 11. Total Closed Catholic School Facility Use by Percentage and by Frequency Count

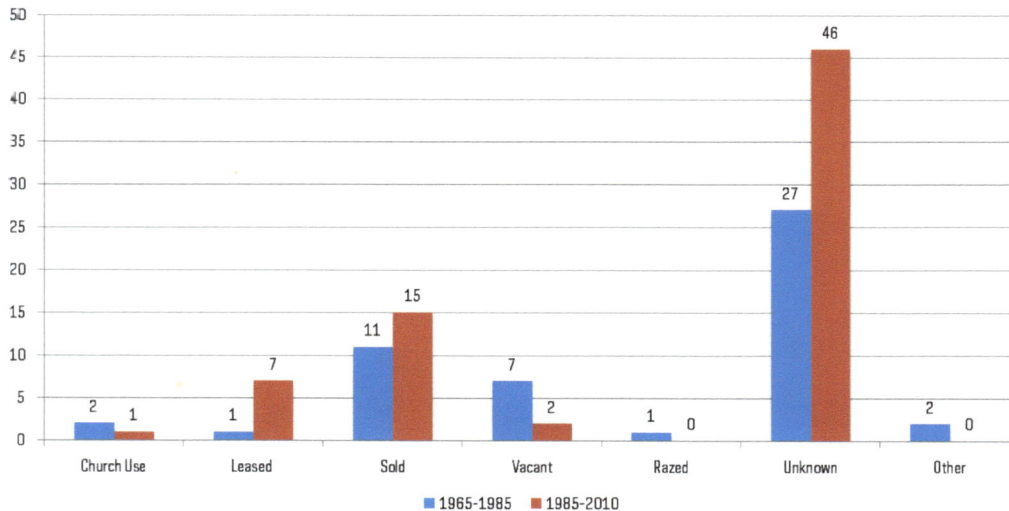

FIGURE D12. Total Catholic School Closures by Decade Window

Notes: One (1) former Catholic school had been leased to a charter school, and one (1) had been sold to the Cleveland Metropolitan School District. However, the limited detail and high number of "unknown" school uses likely means there are others unaccounted for here.

ARCHDIOCESE OF LOUISVILLE

Total School Closures: 97

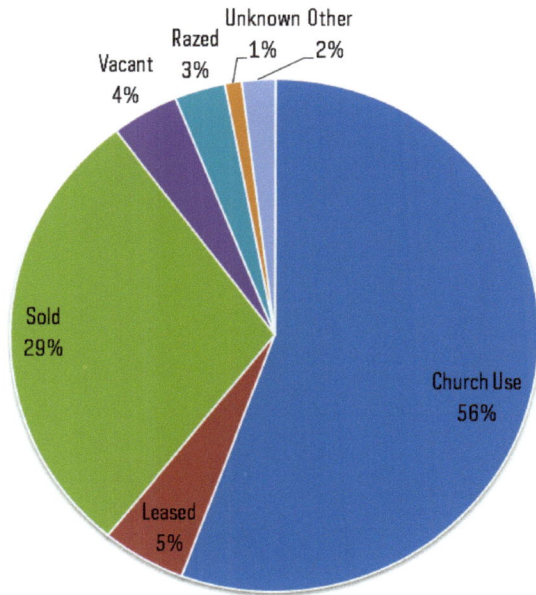

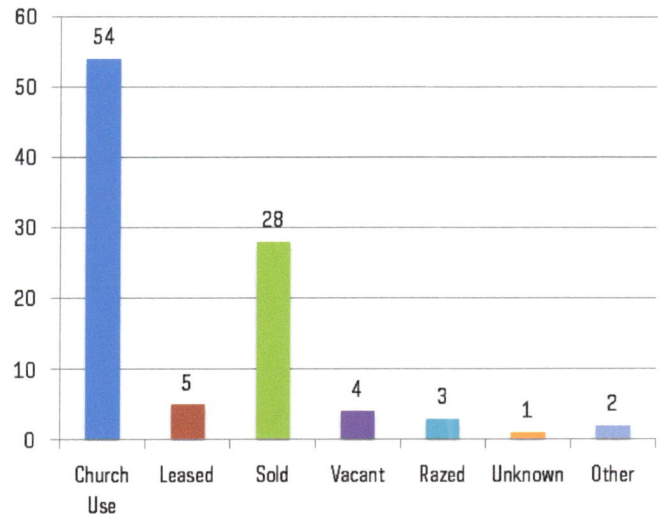

FIGURES D13 and D14. Total Closed Catholic School Facility Use by Percentage and by Frequency Count

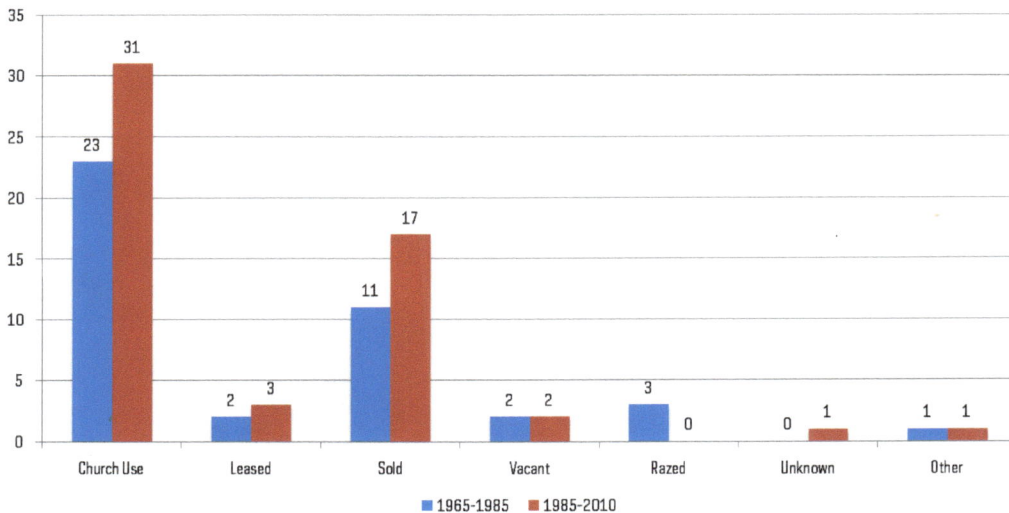

FIGURE D15. Total Catholic School Closures by Decade Window

Notes: The majority of former Catholic school buildings remain under the ownership of the parish for general "Church Use." One (1) former Catholic school had been leased to a Christian school, and one (1) had been sold to a day care provider. No (0) charter sales or leases.

ARCHDIOCESE OF MILWAUKEE

Total School Closures: 131

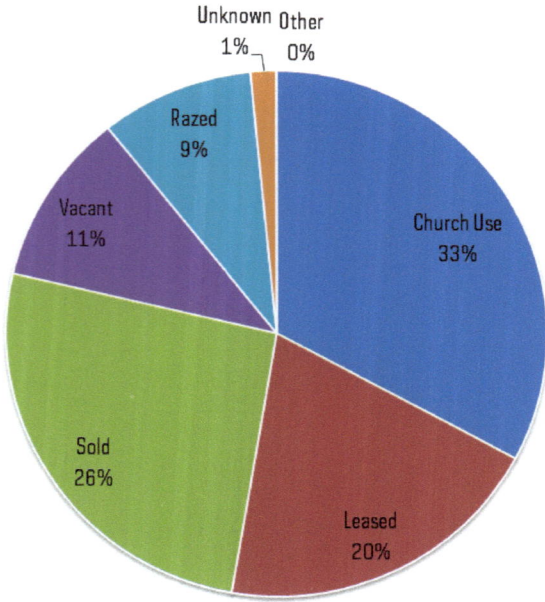

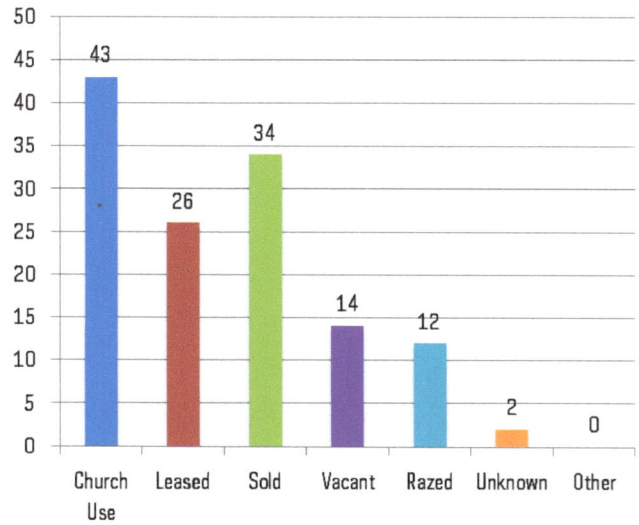

FIGURES D16 and D17. Total Closed Catholic School Facility Use by Percentage and by Frequency Count

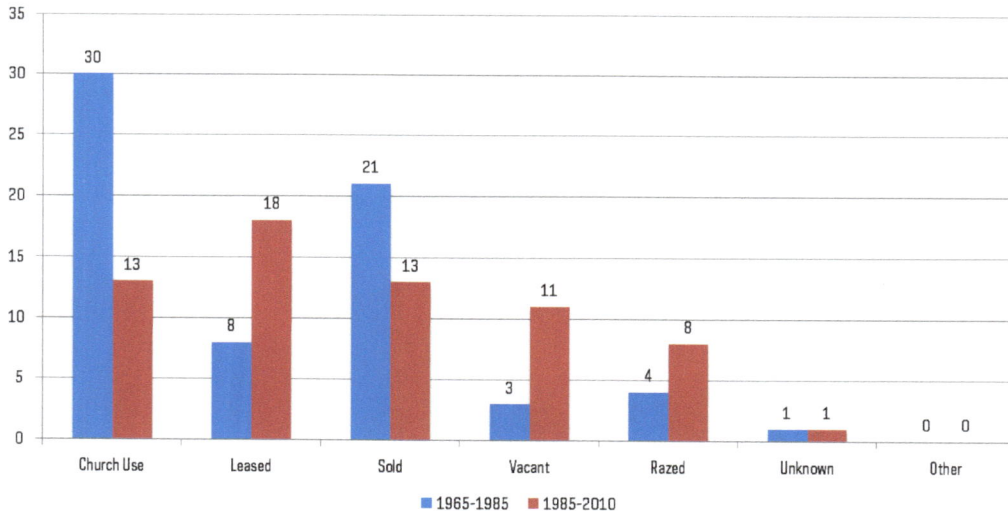

FIGURE D18. Total Catholic School Closures by Decade Window

Notes: Two (2) former Catholic schools had been leased to charter schools, one (1) had been sold to a charter operator, and a total of thirty-four (34) had been leased or sold to educational institutions such as day care providers, Milwaukee Public Schools, and other Christian organizations.

ARCHDIOCESE OF NEWARK

Total School Closures: 178

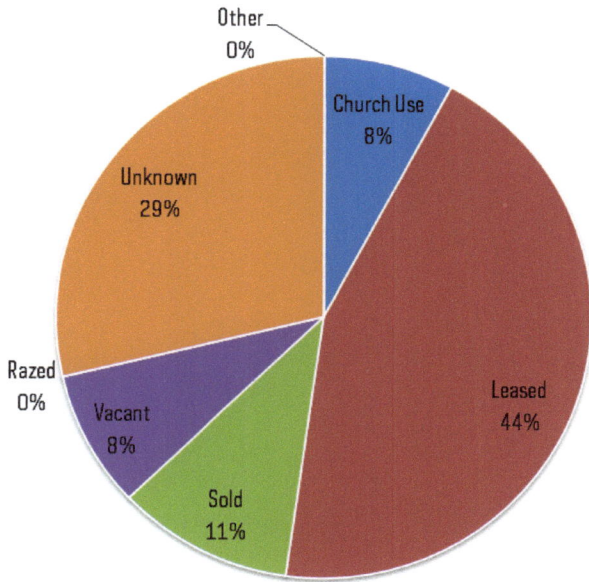

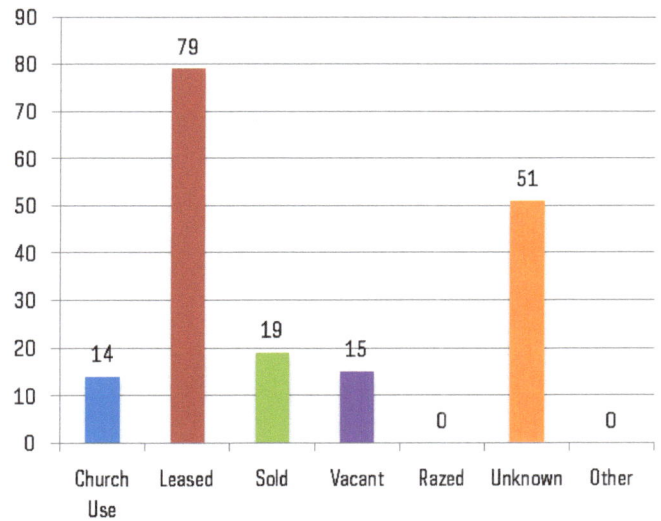

FIGURES D19 and D20. Total Closed Catholic School Facility Use by Percentage and by Frequency Count

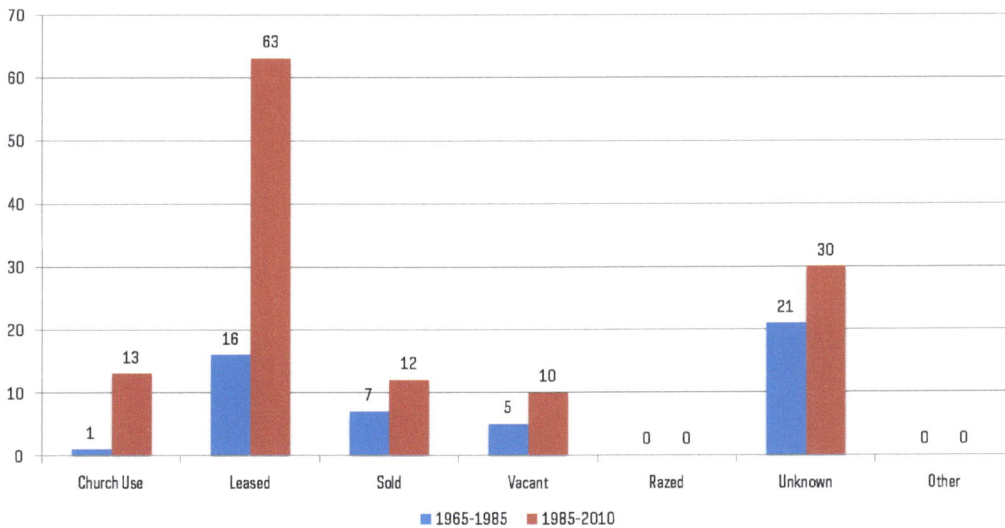

FIGURE D21. Total Catholic School Closures by Decade Window

Notes: Thirteen (13) former Catholic schools had been leased to charter schools, and a total of fifty-nine (59) former Catholic school buildings had been leased to educational institutions. The high number of "unknown" school uses likely means there are others unaccounted for here.

ARCHDIOCESE OF PHILADELPHIA

Total School Closures: 187

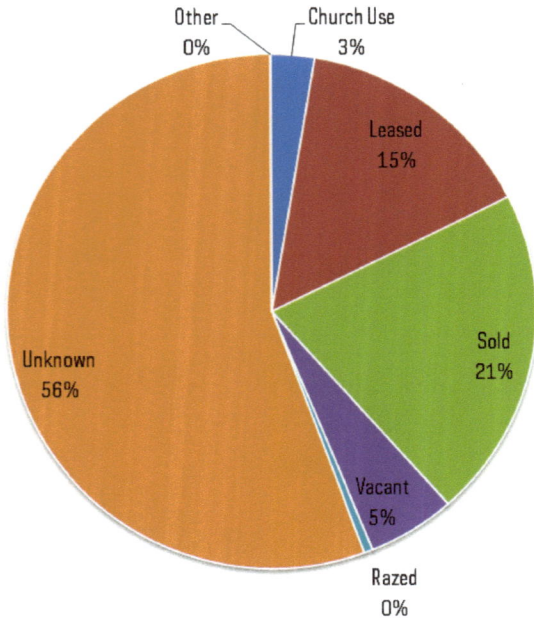

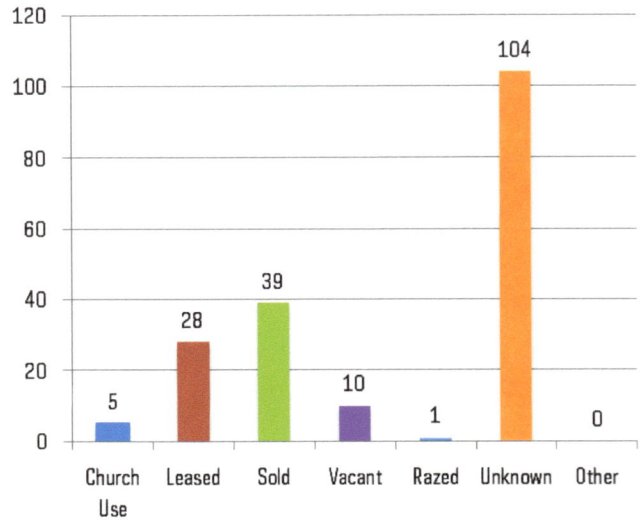

FIGURES D22 and D23. Total Closed Catholic School Facility Use by Percentage and by Frequency Count

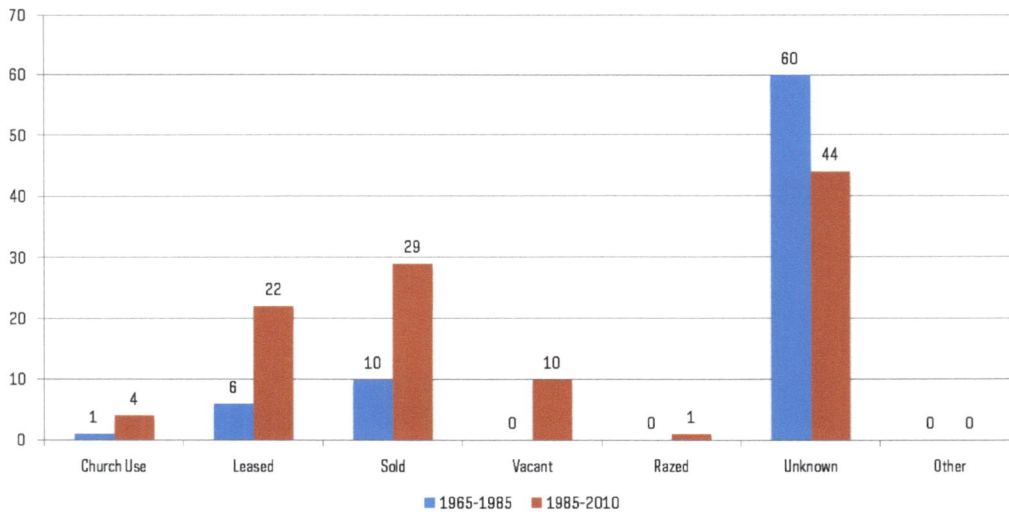

FIGURE D24. Total Catholic School Closures by Decade Window

Notes: Philadelphia provided insufficient data on the specific use of facilities beyond the broad categorical assignment indicated above.

DIOCESE OF SPRINGFIELD, MA

Total School Closures: 50

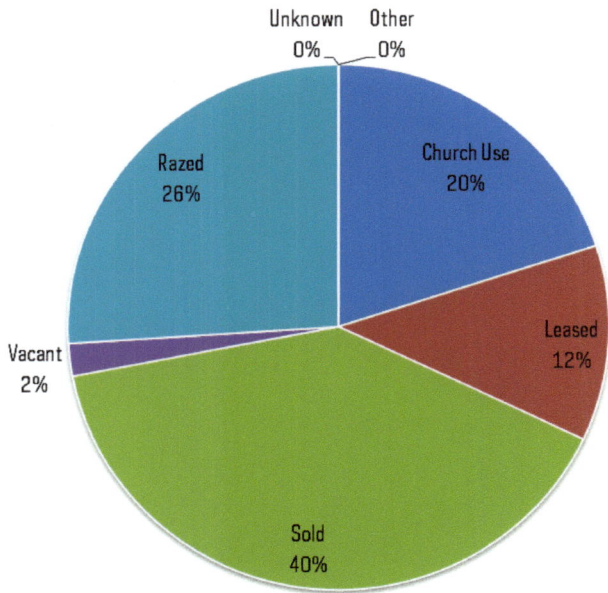

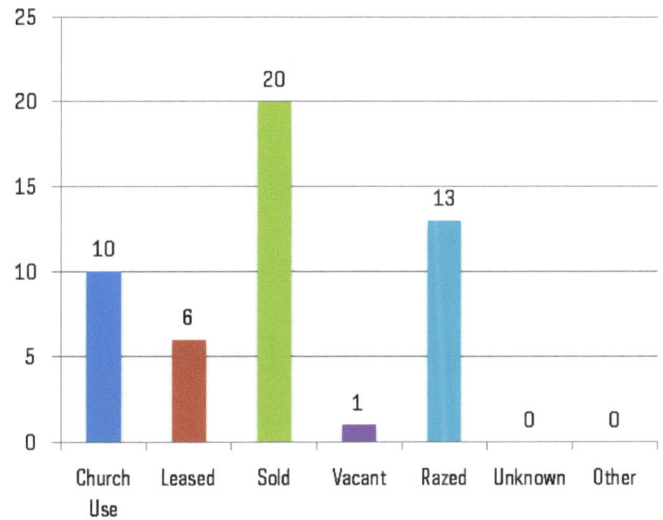

FIGURES D25 and D26. Total Closed Catholic School Facility Use by Percentage and by Frequency Count

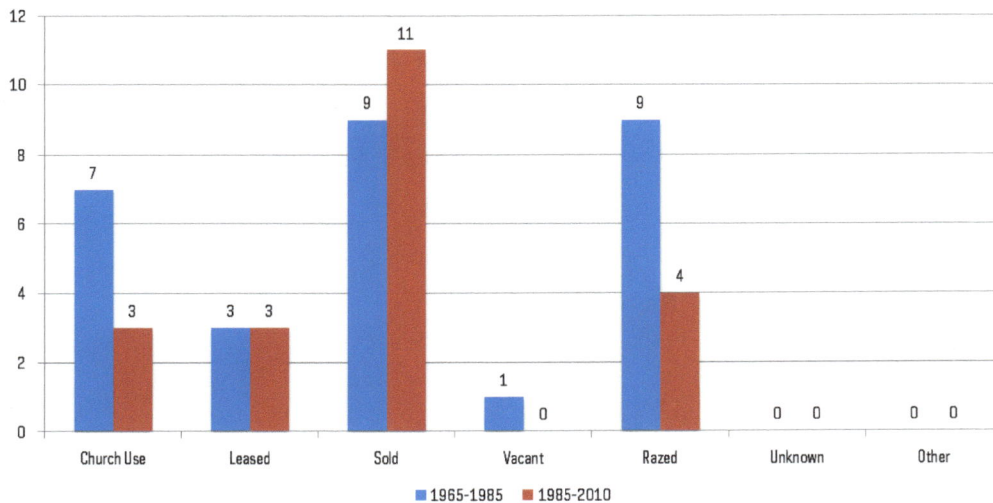

FIGURE D27. Total Catholic School Closures by Decade Window

Notes: All schools were accounted for in the Diocese of Springfield, MA. One (1) former Catholic school had been leased to a charter school. Overall, five (5) former Catholic school buildings had been leased and seven (7) had been sold to educational institutions.

APPENDIX E
Photographic Record of Closed Catholic School Facility Usage

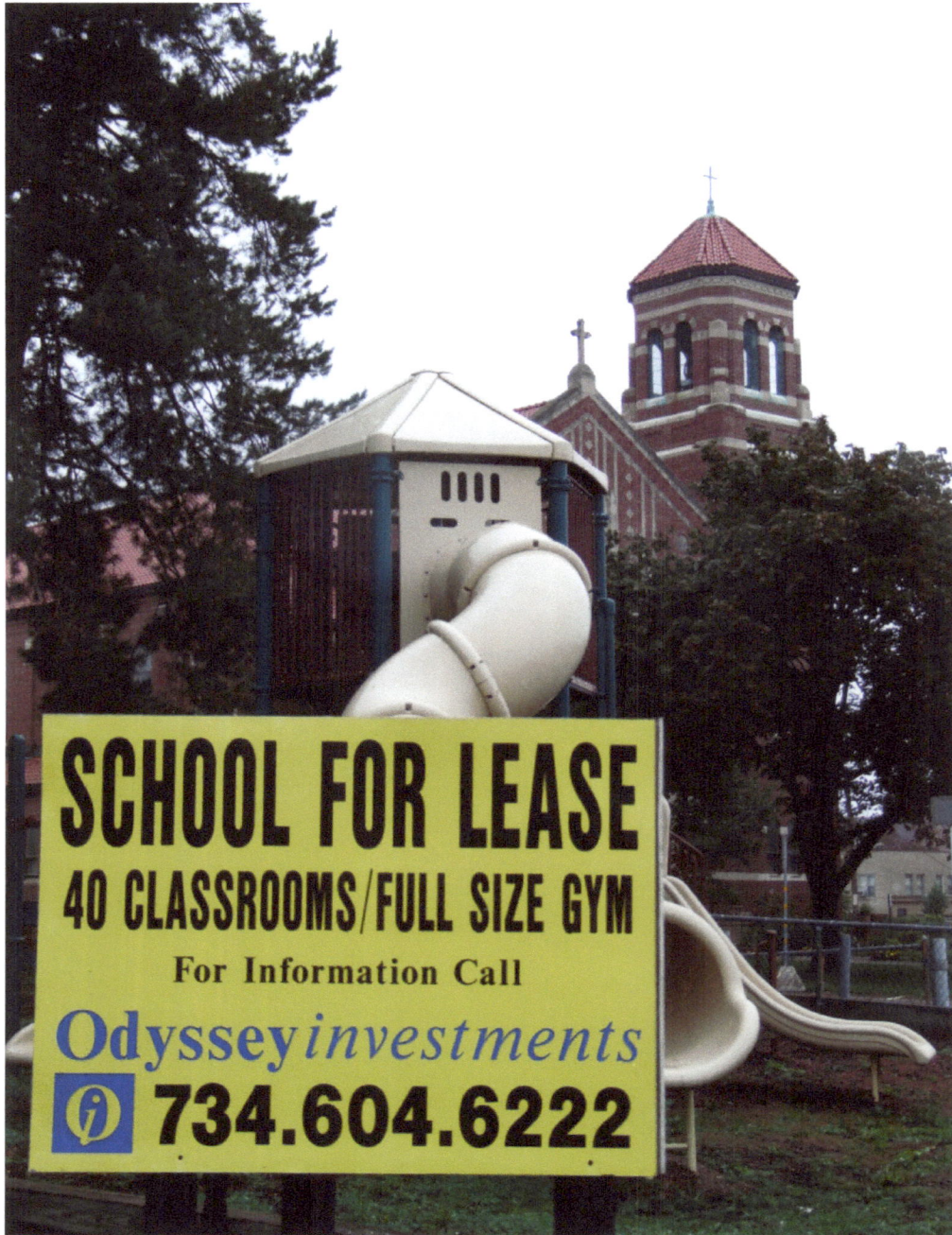

FIGURE E1. Signage in Ferndale, Michigan, just outside Detroit, advertising the lease of an adjacent structure dating to 1925, which served as St. James School. The background depicts the bell tower and church of St. James Catholic Community.

FIGURE E2. This two-story brick building on the corner of N. 36th Street and North Avenue in Milwaukee, formerly St. Anne School, is now home to a local market, Bill the Butcher, Ribs, USA.

FIGURE E3. Hmong American Academy (left) and Grace Hmong Alliance Church now occupy the space of the former St. Lawrence Church and School in Milwaukee. The shadow visible in the picture is cast from St. Joseph Center, the motherhouse of the U.S. Province of the School Sisters of St. Francis.

FIGURE E4. Now serving as the Gary J. Greenfield Administration Building at Wisconsin Lutheran College in Milwaukee, the building and grounds were once the site of the House of the Good Shepherd School.

FIGURE E5. The glass-enclosed elevated walkway connects the former St. Mary School (foreground, right) with the Greektown Casino-Hotel in Detroit. The school structure is a designated Michigan historical site, noted as one of the oldest Catholic school buildings in the state, dating to 1868.

FIGURE E6. In Brooklyn, Mary McDowell Friends School is a Quaker school for students with learning disabilities. St. Charles Borromeo Church (left, background) and parish operated St. Charles Borromeo School at the same site from 1850 to 2006.

FIGURE E7. Despite its façade with religious overtones, capped by a cross at its peak, this structure now houses William A. Butler P.S. 133K in Brooklyn, a public school operated by the New York City Department of Education.

FIGURE E8. These two signs occupy the small green space in front of St. Hilary Catholic Church in Redford, Michigan, a few miles west of Detroit. The building that formerly served as the parish school until 1992 is now home to Detroit West Preparatory Academy.

FIGURE E9. The community room at St. John Neumann Place, a gathering place now frequented by seniors, once had seniors of a different age walking through this space; these windows were the doorways of the high school's main front entrance.

FIGURE E10. In South Philadelphia, a 180-bed skilled nursing facility, St. Monica Manor, is located in the former Our Lady of Mount Carmel Elementary School. The wooden floors and high ceiling of the school gymnasium have been refurbished into a recently dedicated chapel for St. Monica's residents.

FIGURE E11. The long corridor wings of this former high school lead to apartments rather than classrooms. To minimize renovation costs when converting Neumann High School into a senior housing facility, students' lockers were left in place; they still stand behind the newly installed drywall of this hallway.

FIGURE E12. In the Port Richmond neighborhood of Philadelphia, the former parish school at Nativity of the Blessed Virgin Mary awaits conversion to a senior independent living residence. This redevelopment project, spearheaded by the Archdiocese's Catholic Health Care Services, is funded by the U.S. Department of Housing and Urban Development.

APPENDIX F

Original Layout of Nativity School and Architectural Renderings for Conversion to Senior Housing

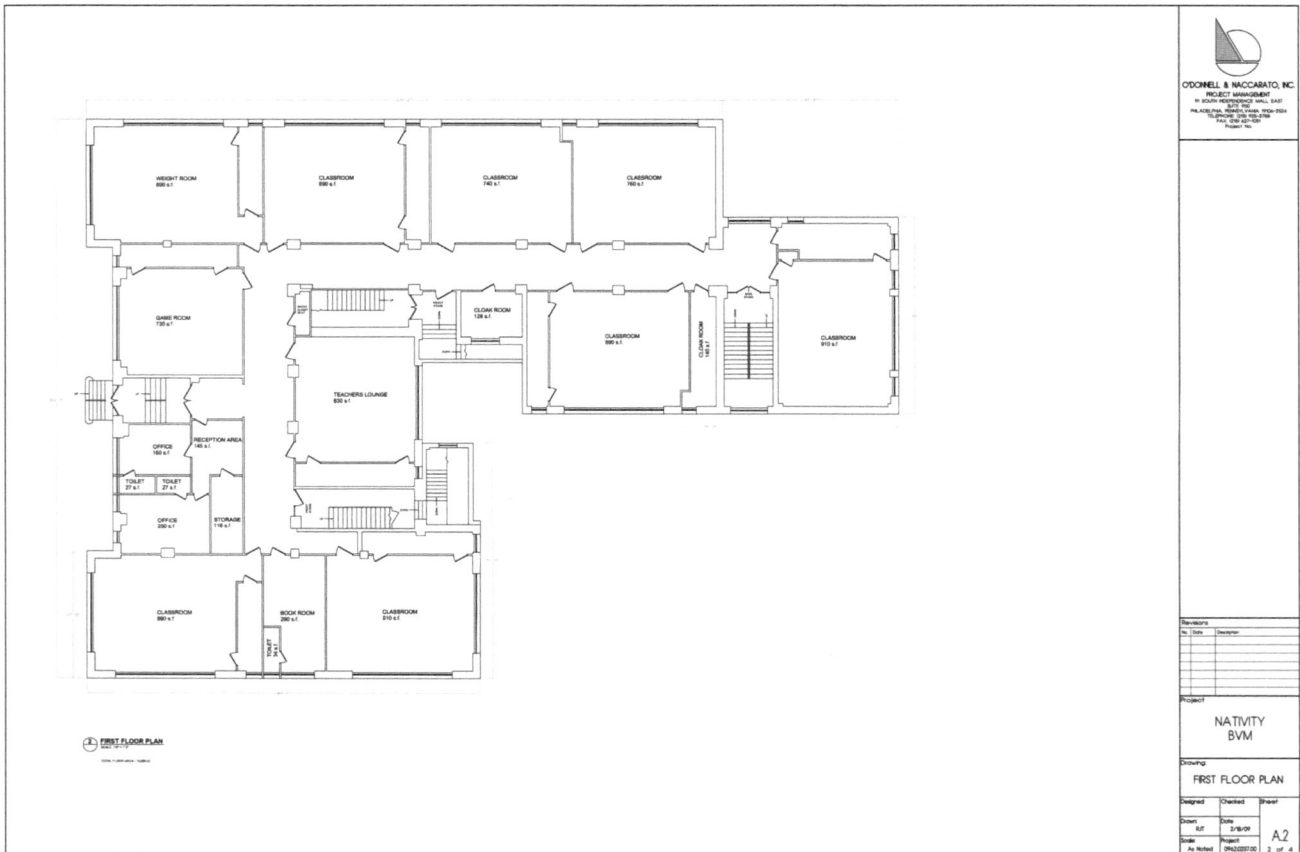

FIGURE F1. First Floor-Existing. Prepared by O'Donnell and Naccarato, Inc. Reprinted with permission.

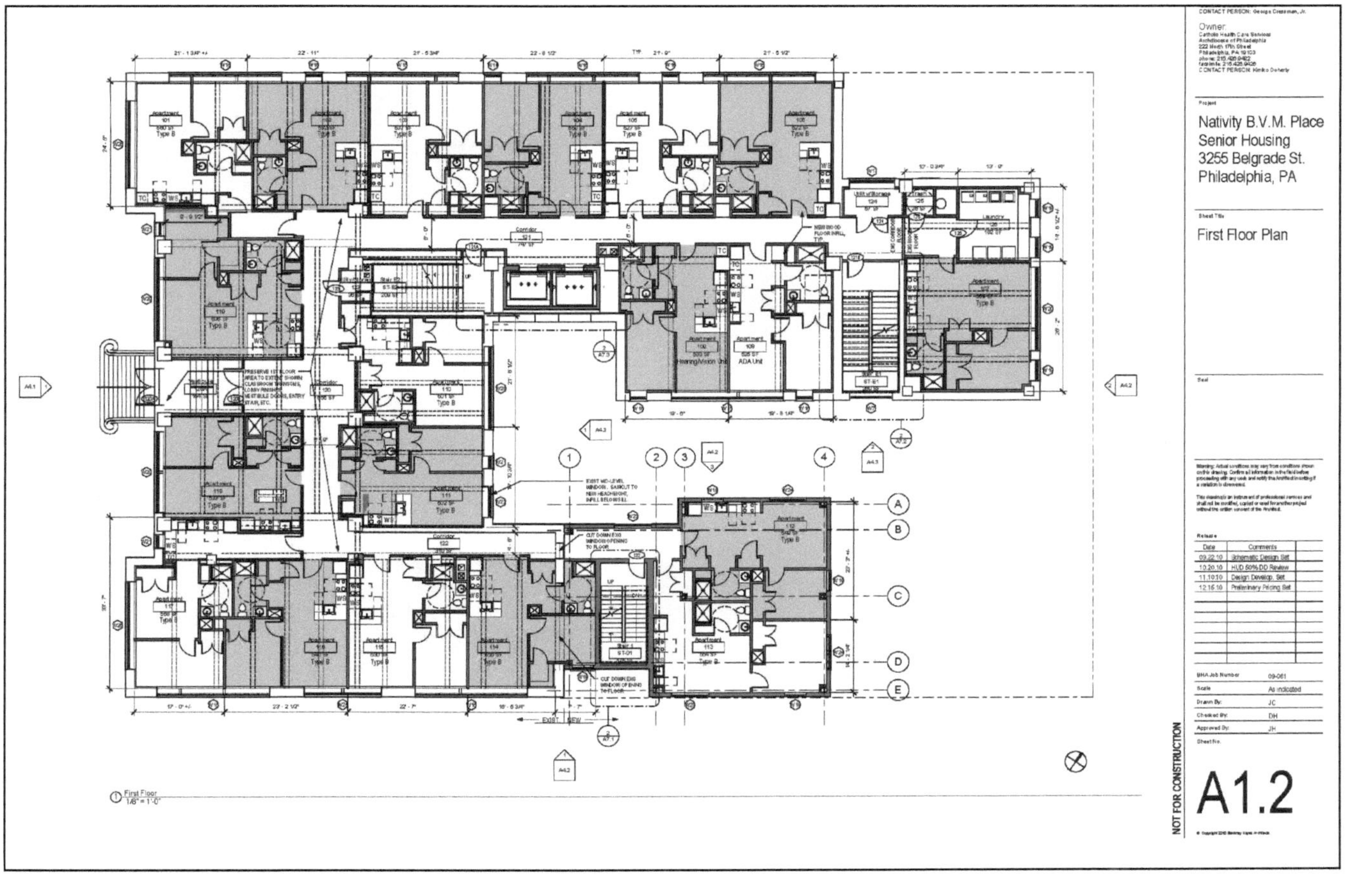

FIGURE F2. First Floor-Proposed. Prepared by Blackney Hayes Architects. Reprinted with permission.

APPENDIX G

Canonical Decree Reaffirming Diocesan Policy Governing the Lease of Ecclesiastical Property to Charter Schools

NICHOLAS DiMARZIO
By the Grace of God and of the Apostolic See
BISHOP OF BROOKLYN

⚜

DECREE

Catholic education is among the many ways in which the Church fulfills its essential teaching function (*munus docendi*), as well as its divine mandate to evangelize. The 1983 Code of Canon law clearly states that, in order for a school to be considered Catholic, it must be directed or recognized by the competent ecclesiastical authority, which for a particular church is the Diocesan Bishop (cf. Can. 803 §1). It goes on to affirm that, "no school is to bear the name *Catholic school* without the consent of competent ecclesiastical authority (Can. 803 §3)." Therefore, by its every definition, a Catholic School exists and functions in communion with the Diocesan Bishop, and can never be considered "independent" of his legitimate authority.

Resulting from this intrinsic communion are several rights afforded to the Diocesan Bishop with respect to Catholic schools in his diocese. For example, the Bishop has the right to appoint and approve, as well as remove teachers of religion in a particular school (Can. 805). Another right afforded the Diocesan Bishop is that of overseeing and visiting all of the Catholic schools in his territory (Can. 806). In addition, the Universal Law affords the Diocesan Bishop the right to issue precepts pertaining to the general regulation of Catholic schools in his diocese (Can. 807).

Therefore, I, the undersigned Bishop of Brooklyn, functioning out of my legitimate authority as diocesan ordinary, and with a desire to correct any erroneous misconceptions, by this canonical decree do hereby reaffirm the diocesan policy governing the leasing of ecclesiastical property to Charter Schools, which has been in place since May 2010. This policy, which is posted on our Diocesan Website, was formulated within the context of our strategic initiative, *Preserving the Vision*, and has as its primary objective the mitigation of any adverse consequences that a potential rental to a Charter School may have on the long term health and viability of its neighboring parochial schools and academies. A constitutive, and, therefore, nonnegotiable part of the aforementioned policy is the revenue sharing of 40% of the proceeds from the rental to those schools which have been identified by the Diocesan Charter School Committee as having been potentially adversely effected by the lease to the Charter School.

This diocesan policy has been in effect since May of 2010 and is binding on all parishes, Catholic schools, as well as all other Catholic institutions in the territory of the Diocese of Brooklyn.

Most Reverend Nicholas DiMarzio, Ph.D., D.D.
Bishop of Brooklyn

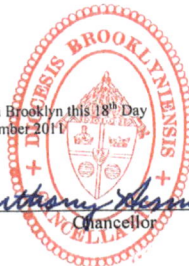

Given in Brooklyn this 18th Day
of November 2011

Chancellor

APPENDIX H
Charter School Rental Guidelines, Diocese of Brooklyn

While it is advantageous for any Catholic institution to rent its vacant property for the long term pastoral and financial support of its pastoral mission, the partial or complete rental of any Catholic facility to a charter school has serious implications for the long term health of the parochial schools and academies of the region. For this reason, no Catholic institution may enter into any lease agreement to rent either its complete facility or a portion of its facility to a charter school without engaging in the process outlined below.

Diocesan Charter School Committee

A Diocesan Charter School Committee will be established to guide the process by which all Catholic institutions located within the territory of the Diocese of Brooklyn may rent a vacant school building or any other facility to a charter school. The Committee will also closely monitor the impact that any charter school rental may have on the surrounding schools/academies of the area and its impact on the pastoral life of the local parishes. Among the members of this committee will be the Vicar General, the Secretary for Catholic Education and Formation, the Vicar for Financial Administration, the Superintendent of Schools (or delegate), the Director of Rocklyn Properties and a representative from the Office of Fiscal Management.

Part of the work of this committee will be to:

- identify strategic placement of future potential charter school rentals;
- monitor the impact that a charter school rental may have upon enrollment trends in the neighboring schools/academies;
- further determine the long term educational and financial impacts such rentals may have upon local schools/academies.

FOUR STEP PROCESS FOR CHARTER SCHOOL RENTAL:

- Step One: Following already established Diocesan guidelines, any pastor or Board Chair that wishes to enter into a rental agreement with a charter school is asked to contact Mrs. Coleen Ceriello of Rocklyn Assets Corporation for assistance in securing possible tenants for the facility in question. These norms must also be employed in those cases when the Diocese wishes to explore the rental of any of its properties to a charter school provider.

- Step Two: If a charter school expresses reasonable interest in renting any Catholic facility, the Pastor of the parish or the Board Chair is asked to submit a written request for permission to the Diocesan Bishop to pursue such a rental.

  A. Parish Process: Before permission can be sought for any vacant facility to be rented to a charter school provider, the pastor is asked to consult with parish leadership in the following manner:

     The Pastor must consult with the Parish Trustees, members of the Finance Council and Parish Pastoral Council to seek their advance on pursuing the rental of the parish school to a charter school.

The agenda for this meeting(s) will include the following:

- Understanding the Charter School Rental
  a. The purpose of the Charter School
  b. Proposed number of classes and students at the time of opening
  c. The educational philosophy of the Charter School
  d. The Charter School application process and its curriculum
  e. The impact of a Charter school rental on neighboring schools/academies

- Discussion of possible impact of the rental on the pastoral life of the parish, if any
- Discussion of possible impact on other properties of the parish, if any
- Financial implications of the rental
  a. Benefit to the parish
  b. Benefit to the Catholic schools in the surrounding area

When the parish consultation is completed, the Pastor is asked to submit a letter to the Bishop seeking permission to pursue the charter school rental. A copy of the official minutes of the parish consultation meeting shall accompany this written request to the Bishop. A copy of both the letter and minutes shall also be sent to the chairperson of the Diocesan Charter School Committee and be retained in the parish's file.

B. All other Catholic institutions: Before permission can be sought for any other Catholic facility to be rented, in whole or part, to a charter school provider, the Board Chair or an equivalent competent authority is asked to consult with the governing body of the respective institution in accordance with the by-laws that govern it.

When this consultation is completed, the Board Chair is asked to submit a letter to the Bishop seeking permission to pursue the charter school rental. A copy of the official minutes of the Board consultation meeting shall accompany this written request to the Bishop.

- Step Three: Once the Bishop has granted permission for a Catholic institution to pursue a charter school rental, the Office of the Superintendent will be asked to complete an analysis needed to give clearance for any proposed charter school rental. This analysis consists of three parts.

  Part One: The Office of the Superintendent will engage the leadership of the local parishes, and schools and academies of the area that will be affected by the charter school rental to solicit their concerns and answer whatever questions they may have about the possible lease.

  Part Two: The Office of the Superintendent will also determine the charter school rental impact by assessing the School District, the area affect by the School District and the schools located within the School District. Further analysis of the student zip code will be done once the School District is determined.

  Part Three: Before any rental agreement to a charter school is finalized, the following two items must be certified by the Superintendent of Schools and presented to the Secretary of Catholic Education and Formation:

  - The Charter School Curriculum must be reviewed ensuring that nothing will be taught in violation of the doctrinal and moral teachings of the Catholic Church.

  - A final list of schools impacted by the rental will be assembled for the Bishop's approval. These schools will be eligible to receive direct financial aid to mitigate the effect of the charter school's presence in the region. Aid will be given through a sharing of 40% of the total rental income to be paid on an annual basis to the charter school to the host parish.

The findings of the Superintendent will be communicated to the Pastor or Board Chair, the Director of Rocklyn Properties and the Chairperson of the Diocesan Charter School Committee.

- Step Four: Upon successful completion of step three and the completion of the final terms of the lease by Rocklyn Properties, including the final rental amount and the schedule for its payment, the Diocesan Charter School Committee will make its recommendation known to the Diocesan Bishop regarding the completion of the proposed rental agreement. After considering the Committee's recommendation, the Diocesan Bishop will inform the competent authority of his final decision regarding the proposed rental.

If permission is granted for a parish to proceed with such a rental, the pastor will complete the rental process under the supervision of Ms. Coleen Ceriello, Director of Rocklyn Properties.

REVENUE SHARING PROCESS AND ASSESSMENT TOOL

- Each year there will be revenue sharing amounting to 40% of the total rental income, to be shared on a per capita basis based on K-8 Enrollment for all the parochial schools/academies of the area, as recommended by the Superintendent of Schools and approved by the Bishop.

- For parishes that rent their facilities to charter schools, they are required to pay their broker fees and complete repayment of past Diocesan debts. In order to achieve this requirement, any such parish that has an outstanding debt to the Diocese of Brooklyn must create a payment plan for approval by the Vicar for Financial Administration.

- The St. Elizabeth Ann Seton Trust will handle all funds generated by the revenue sharing of charter school rentals. Contributions into the Trust will be made in four equal installments each year. These installments will be due December 1st, March 1st, June 1st, and August 15th. The Trust will disburse to the school in two equal payments during the academic year. The first payment will be sent on January 30th and the second will be made on April 30th.

- Beginning in the second year of the lease, documentation of actual Student Loss will be monitored by the Office of the Superintendent, allowing more targeted aid for those schools experiencing a more severe impact from the charter school.

- Provide a percentage of the rental revenue up front based on student loss. This will allow for the creation of a formula based on the actual per pupil costs and the rate of loss on the school to adjust future revenue sharing among the schools of the area.

- Each school receiving financial aid will be asked to determine the specific use of the revenue sharing funds it will receive and will need to evaluate the success of the use of the revenue sharing in meeting its stated goals.

APPENDIX I

Self-Assessment Checklist
for (Arch)Diocesan Best Practices

PRACTICES	STATUS		
	Not in Place	In Progress	In Place
PERSONNEL Central office personnel designated to collect, organize, and make available all property-related information	☐	☐	☐
EXISTING POLICY Diocesan policy in place for the management of all closed school and other unused facilities	☐	☐	☐
REPORTING PROPERTY INFORMATION Standard reporting mechanism published and distributed for cataloging and evaluating property-related information	☐	☐	☐
DATABASE FOR PROPERTY INFORMATION Database and/or website created for archiving property-related information, including detailed descriptions and architectural plans, a current, professional physical plant assessment detailing strengths and weaknesses, a maintenance plan with estimated costs, onsite manager contact information, and a photographic record	☐	☐	☐
DATA-INFORMED DECISION MAKING Database and/or website made available and utilized during decision-making processes diocesan-wide	☐	☐	☐
VETTING OF POTENTIAL RENTERS Thorough vetting of potential renters or purchasers of property to assure compatibility with the teachings and practices of the Catholic Church	☐	☐	☐
BROAD CONSULTATION Broad consultation with all affected stakeholders, including pastors and parish leaders, regarding the proposed repurposing of any facility	☐	☐	☐
RETIREMENT OF OUTSTANDING DEBTS Outstanding diocesan debts retired first with any income from property sale or lease	☐	☐	☐

PRACTICES	STATUS		
	Not in Place	In Progress	In Place
EVALUATION OF IMPACT Comprehensive evaluation of the impact of any lease or sale on current Catholic schools and other church sponsored educational programs	☐	☐	☐
DIOCESAN ASSESSMENT Institution of a diocesan tax on rental and sale income for the purpose of funding tuition scholarships to Catholic schools for students with demonstrated need	☐	☐	☐
GUIDELINES FOR ALIENATION OF PROPERTY Careful consideration of the dictates of canon law and local diocesan legislation regarding the disposition and alienation of property, including the enactment of deed restrictions	☐	☐	☐
FULL DISCLOSURE Fully disclose terms of any leases and sales	☐	☐	☐
PROFESSIONAL CONSULTATION Secure appropriate professional expertise in the razing of any facility, with special attention to risk management, safety, asbestos abatement, and site preparation	☐	☐	☐
STRATEGIC PLANNING INCLUDES FACILITIES DATA Include comprehensive information on unused facilities in diocesan strategic planning	☐	☐	☐

ABOUT THE AUTHORS

REV. RONALD J. NUZZI is a priest of the Diocese of Youngstown, Ohio. He is Senior Director of The Mary Ann Remick Leadership Program in the Alliance for Catholic Education at the University of Notre Dame, where he leads a dedicated graduate program to prepare principals for service in Catholic schools. A nationally known speaker and scholar, Nuzzi has led dozens of staff development days, in-services, and retreats for Catholic school teachers and administrators in the United States, Canada, Mexico, Australia, and Italy. He has published widely, including several research handbooks and an encyclopedia, all focused on Catholic education. He holds a Ph.D. in Educational Administration from the University of Dayton and Master's degrees in Philosophy, Theology, and Education.

JAMES M. FRABUTT is Faculty in The Mary Ann Remick Leadership Program in the Alliance for Catholic Education and Concurrent Associate Professor of Psychology at the University of Notre Dame. With colleagues in the Remick Leadership Program, he has co-authored two books, *Research, Action, and Change: Leaders Reshaping Catholic Schools*, and *Faith, Finances, and the Future: The Notre Dame Study of U.S. Pastors*. He has employed action-oriented, community-based research approaches to areas such as juvenile delinquency prevention, school-based mental health, teacher/administrator inquiry, racial disparities in the juvenile justice system, and community violence reduction. He holds a B.A. in Psychology and Italian from the University of Notre Dame and a Master's degree and Ph.D. in Human Development and Family Studies from the University of North Carolina at Greensboro.

ANTHONY C. HOLTER is Faculty in The Mary Ann Remick Leadership Program in the Alliance for Catholic Education and Concurrent Assistant Professor of Psychology at the University of Notre Dame. Holter recently co-authored *Research, Action, and Change: Leaders Reshaping Catholic Schools* with colleagues in the Remick Leadership Program, highlighting his interest in examining how sound educational research methods support and animate core tenets of the Catholic faith tradition. Holter also conducts research on effective measures of Catholic identity for Catholic schools. He holds a B.A. in Theology and Humanities from Saint Mary's University of Minnesota, a Master's degree in Education from the University of Notre Dame, and a Master's degree and Ph.D. in Educational Psychology from the University of Wisconsin —Madison.

Correspondence concerning this study should be addressed to Rev. Ronald J. Nuzzi, Ph.D., University of Notre Dame, 107 Carole Sandner Hall, Notre Dame, IN 46556.